AF730572

HIDDEN PROFESSIONS

CAREERS THAT SURVIVE AI
(AND DON'T REQUIRE A DEGREE)

BY
J.S. HODGE

A BLUE NEBULA BOOKS FIRST EDITION

HIDDEN PROFESSIONS
Careers that Survive AI
(And Don't Require a Degree)

Copyright © 2025 by J.S.HODGE

All rights reserved. No part of this book may be reproduced or transmitted in any form or by any means, both known and unknown, electronic or mechanical, including photocopying, recording, or by any information storage and retrieval system, without express written permission from the Publisher, with the exception of brief quotes used in connection with reviews for any written, audio or visual media.

All information contained is current as of January 2026. Salaries and requirements vary based upon location and demand. Readers interested in a given field are encouraged to contact regional or state boards for further information.

LIBRARY OF CONGRESS
205927960

ISBN: 978-0-9842436-9-3

Published in the United States by
Blue Nebula Books
Otter Rock, OR

This book is dedicated to those
hoping to find their place
in this world.

Author's Note

This book was not written out of resentment toward education, technology, or progress. I am not anti-education nor am I anti-technology. I am not nostalgic for some imagined past where work was purer or simpler. I have benefited from formal education, professional credentials, and decades of technical work myself.

This book exists for a different reason.

Over time, I began to notice how many essential careers had quietly disappeared from public conversation—not because they vanished, but because they were no longer fashionable to discuss. Work that kept people alive, kept systems running, and kept risk contained was still being done every day, but rarely acknowledged as a career path, much less a dignified one.

At the same time, I watched the language around work narrow. Success became synonymous with visibility. Intelligence became synonymous with elitism. Worth became increasingly detached from consequence. And many capable people—experienced, steady, and competent—were left feeling obsolete, not because their skills no longer mattered, but because the culture stopped noticing them.

This book is a corrective to that distortion.

The professions described here are not theoretical. They are not speculative. They are not future bets. They exist now, in every region of the country, staffed by people whose names rarely appear in headlines precisely because their work prevents crises rather than responding to them.

I did not choose these careers to make an argument against artificial intelligence. I chose them because they reveal something more important: where responsibility still resides.

Technology changes how work is done. It does not change the fact that someone must be accountable when things go wrong. In medicine, infrastructure, industry, safety, and logistics, that accountability remains stubbornly human.

If this book has a point of view, it is a simple one: usefulness does not expire on a predictable schedule. Many forms of meaningful work are hidden not because they are unimportant, but because they are quiet, regulated, and resistant to hype.

This book is for people reassessing their relationship to work—not just how to earn, but how to endure. It is for those considering a second act, or simply seeking something sturdier than constant reinvention.

If you recognize yourself in these pages, I hope this book helps you see options that were always there—but rarely named. And if you never pursue any of these paths, I hope you come away with a renewed respect for the people who do.

They are holding more together than most of us realize.

TABLE OF CONTENTS

INTRODUCTION.......................................1

CHAPTER 1. HEALTHCARE
Where Human Presence Still Matters.......15

PROFILE 1:
BOARD CERTIFIED
INSTRUMENT SPECIALIST............17

PROFILE 2:
OPHTHALMIC TECHNICIAN.......21

PROFILE 3:
SLEEP TECHNOLOGIST.................25

PROFILE 4:
NEURODIAGNOSTIC
TECHNOLOGIST..............................29

PROFILE 5:
DIALYSIS TECHNICIAN 33

PROFILE 6:
RESPIRATORY THERAPY
ASSISTANT..37

PROFILE 7:
PULMONARY FUNCTION
TECHNICIAN.......................................41

TABLE OF CONTENTS (CONTINUED)

CHAPTER 2: INFRASTRUCTURE:
The Work That Holds Society Together..........47

PROFILE 8
WATER TREATMENT PLANT OPERATOR..51

PROFILE 9
ELECTRICAL LINE WORKER..............55

PROFILE 10
POWER PLANT OPERATOR.................59

PROFILE 11
SUBSTATION TECHNICIAN.................63

PROFILE 12
ELEVATOR MECHANIC..........................67

PROFILE 13
BUILDING INSPECTOR..........................71

PROFILE 14
SURVEY TECHNICIAN...........................75

TABLE OF CONTENTS (CONTINUED)

CHAPTER 3: MUNICIPAL CAREERS
The Professions That Keep
Civilization Running..................................83

PROFILE 15
FIREFIGHTER..................................85

PROFILE 16:
POLICE OFFICER............................91

PROFILE 17:
EMERGENCY MANAGEMENT
OFFICIAL..97

PROFILE 18:
CODE ENFORCEMENT
OFFICER..103

PROFILE 19:
SANITARIAN......................................109

PROFILE 20:
PARKS MANAGER...........................115

TABLE OF CONTENTS (CONTINUED)

CHAPTER 4: INDUSTRY AND FIELD SYSTEMS
Where Reality Pushes Back......................123

PROFILE 21
HEAVY EQUIPMENT FIELD TECHNICIAN....................................125

PROFILE 22:
INDUSTRIAL INSTRUMENTATION TECHNICIAN....................................129

PROFILE 23:
PIPELINE OPERATOR...................133

PROFILE 24:
MILLWRIGHT...................................137

PROFILE 25:
BOILER OPERATOR......................141

PROFILE 26:
INDUSTRIAL TECHNICIAN.......145

TABLE OF CONTENTS (CONTINUED)

CHAPTER 5: ENVIRONMENT, SAFETY AND REGULATION
Where Risk is Managed, Not Eliminated.......................................153

PROFILE 27
ENVIRONMENTAL HEALTH AND SAFETY TECHNICIAN........157

PROFILE 28:
HAZARDOUS MATERIAL TECHNICIAN......................................161

PROFILE 29:
ENVIRONMENTAL COMPLIANCE INSPECTOR...165

PROFILE 30:
INDUSTRIAL HYGIENE TECHNICIAN......................................169

PROFILE 31:
FIRE INSPECTOR.............................173

TABLE OF CONTENTS (CONTINUED)

CHAPTER 6: LOGISTICS, MOVEMENT, AND SYSTEM CONTROLS
Where Flow is Everything........................179

PROFILE 32
RAILROAD DISPATCHER 181

PROFILE 33:
AIR TRAFFIC CONTROLLER.....185

PROFILE 34:
PORT OPERATIONS COORDINATOR.............................189

PROFILE 35:
SCADA. CONTROL ROOM OPERATOR.......................................193

PROFILE 36:
TRANSPORTATION OPERATIONS COORDINATOR.............................197

CHAPTER 7: SECOND ACTS AND SUSTAINABLE CAREERS.
Who Are These Positions for?..........203

CHAPTER 8: CHOOSING WORK THAT ENDURES...................................209

Introduction

The Careers We Forgot to Talk About

For decades, young people in America have been told a remarkably consistent story: Work hard in high school, go to college, earn a degree, and a meaningful career will follow.

For many, that path worked. For many others, it didn't.

Student debt ballooned. Degrees multiplied. Jobs that once offered dignity and stability became automated, outsourced, or stripped of long-term security. At the same time, millions of capable people—curious, practical, and motivated—found themselves excluded from opportunity not by lack of ability, but by cost, time, or an unwillingness to gamble their future on debt.

What rarely gets discussed is this: there exists an entire ecosystem of legitimate, regulated, often well-paid professions that sit quietly outside the college-industrial narrative. These are not "fallback jobs." They are not "unskilled labor." They are not temporary gigs. They are careers, some with decades-long track records, requiring focused training, certification, apprenticeships, licensing, and professional ethics. Many serve critical roles in healthcare, infrastructure, public safety, environmental protection, and specialized technical services. Some are recession-resistant. Some are portable. Some allow individuals to work independently or build small businesses. Many provide something increasingly rare: a sense of usefulness.

Yet most people never hear about them.

High school counselors don't mention them. Career fairs ignore them. Popular media rarely profiles them. And online job platforms often bury them beneath degree filters that have little to do with actual job performance. This book exists to correct that blind spot.

Hidden Professions is a practical guide to careers that typically only require:

- A high school diploma or equivalent,
- Targeted training (often online or vocational),
- State, local, or national certification or licensure.

Each profile in this book focuses on:

- What the profession actually does,
- How someone enters the field,
- Typical training costs and time commitments,
- Certification and regulatory requirements,
- Income ranges and long-term viability, and,
- The kind of person who tends to thrive in the role.

This is not an argument against education.

It is an argument against the assumption that there is only one respectable path forward.

Some people want to build things. Some want to fix them. Some want to serve quietly and competently. Some want work that ends when the day ends. Others want autonomy, mobility, or purpose more than prestige.

All of those goals are valid.

If you are a student trying to avoid crushing debt, a mid-career adult looking for reinvention, a retiree seeking meaningful part-time work, or simply someone who suspects that the career conversation has been artificially narrowed—this book is for you.

The professions described here have always existed.

They were never deliberately hidden. We just stopped talking about them.

Why Degrees Became Gatekeepers

College degrees were not always career gatekeepers. For much of the twentieth century, employers used degrees as signals, not barriers. A degree suggested literacy, discipline, and exposure to ideas—but it was rarely treated as proof of job readiness. Training happened on the job. Skills were taught by doing. Credentials followed experience, not the other way around.

That changed gradually, then all at once.

As higher education expanded after World War II, degrees became more common. As they became more common, their signaling power diminished. Employers responded not by questioning the relevance of degrees, but by raising the bar. Jobs that once required a high school diploma began to require an associate's degree. Associate-level roles began demanding bachelor's degrees. Eventually, entire categories of work quietly absorbed degree requirements that had little relationship to actual performance.

This process—often called credential inflation—was not driven by conspiracy or malice. It was driven by convenience.

Degrees became an efficient filter.

Faced with hundreds or thousands of applicants, employers discovered that requiring a degree dramatically reduced the pool. Human resources departments adopted degree requirements as a risk-management tool, not a skills assessment. Automated hiring systems followed suit, embedding educational thresholds into software that often no longer reflected the realities of the work itself.

At the same time, institutions of higher education adapted to demand. Programs proliferated. Tuition rose. Marketing departments reframed college not as one path among many, but as the only path to legitimacy. The result was a feedback loop: employers expected degrees because applicants had them, and applicants pursued degrees because employers expected them.

What was lost in the process was proportionality.

A degree became a proxy for competence, even when competence could be demonstrated more directly through training, certification, or supervised practice. Entire professions—particularly those involving hands-on, technical, or interpersonal work—were pushed to the margins of the career conversation, despite remaining essential to society.

Meanwhile, the cost of participation rose sharply.

Time spent earning degrees increased. Debt became normalized. Opportunity costs—the years of no earnings, not building experience, not exploring alternatives—were reframed as necessary sacrifices. For many, the gamble paid off. For many others, it did not.

The problem is not that degrees lack value. The problem is that degrees became default credentials for jobs that do not require them, while alternative pathways were quietly de-legitimized.

This shift had consequences:

- Capable people were excluded before they could demonstrate skill
- Employers confused formal education with job readiness
- Trades, technical, and certification-based careers lost cultural visibility
- Work that once offered dignity without debt was mislabeled as lesser

In this environment, choosing a non-degree path began to look like failure rather than intention.

That perception is false.

The professions profiled in this book exist precisely because degrees are not the only way to establish trust, competence, and accountability. Licensing boards, certifying bodies, apprenticeships, and continuing education requirements often provide more relevant oversight than generalized academic credentials. These systems are narrower, stricter, and closer to the actual work.

Understanding how degrees became gatekeepers

is not about assigning blame. It is about restoring balance—and recognizing that the labor market did not become more complex because more diplomas were issued. It became more complex because society stopped valuing multiple forms of expertise.

The chapters that follow are an invitation to reopen that conversation.

Who This Book Is For.

This book is for people who suspect that the career map they were handed is incomplete.

It is for students who are capable, curious, and practical—but unwilling to accept crushing debt as the price of entry into adult life. For those who want to work, earn, and build competence sooner rather than later, without being told they have somehow "settled."

It is for mid-career adults who did what they were supposed to do, followed the rules, earned credentials, and still found themselves underutilized, displaced, or quietly dissatisfied. For people who are less interested in status than in usefulness, stability, or autonomy.

It is for retirees and near-retirees who are not finished contributing, but who want work that is meaningful without being consuming—roles where experience, patience, and reliability matter more than résumés optimized for algorithms.

It is for parents, counselors, mentors, and educators who want to offer realistic guidance rather than inherited assumptions. For those who understand that a single narrative cannot serve every temperament, learning style, or life circumstance.

And it is for anyone who values competence

over credentials, responsibility over prestige, and contribution over title.

This book is not anti-education.

It does not argue that college is useless, that degrees are fraudulent, or that intellectual study lacks value. It does not dismiss professions that require advanced academic training, nor does it promise shortcuts to wealth or effort-free success.

What it does reject is the idea that intelligence, worth, or ambition can be reliably inferred from the presence—or absence—of a diploma.

The careers described here require real commitment. Many involve licensing exams, supervised training, continuing education, regulatory oversight, and professional accountability. Some demand emotional resilience. Some require technical precision. Others require patience, judgment, and a willingness to work quietly without applause.

They are not easy paths. They are simply different ones.

If you are looking for a catalog of "get rich quick" schemes, this book is not for you. If you believe that meaningful work must be validated by prestige alone, it may challenge you. If you are open to the possibility that purpose can be found outside familiar hierarchies—and that stability can exist without lifelong debt—you are exactly who this book was written for.

The profiles that follow are not prescriptions. They are options.

You decide which, if any, belong in your life.

Certification, Licensure, and Trust

Every profession, whether openly acknowledged or not, exists to solve a problem of trust.

When a stranger installs wiring in your home, adjusts a medical device, inspects a bridge, or certifies drinking water as safe, you are placing your well-being in their hands. Society cannot function if every individual must personally verify the competence of every professional they encounter. Trust must be transferable.

Degrees are one way of attempting to solve this problem—but they are not the only way, nor always the best way.

In many of the professions covered in this book, trust is established through certification and licensure, not academic credentials. These systems are narrower in scope, closer to the actual work, and often more rigorous in ongoing accountability than generalized degree programs.

Certification typically indicates that an individual has demonstrated competence in a defined set of skills or knowledge areas. Licensure goes further: it grants legal authority to practice, backed by regulatory oversight, ethical standards, and the possibility of revocation. In both cases, trust is not assumed—it is earned, tested, and maintained.

These frameworks tend to share several features:

- Clearly defined competencies tied directly to job tasks
- Standardized examinations or supervised training requirements
- Continuing education to maintain relevance and safety

- Disciplinary mechanisms for misconduct or negligence

Unlike degrees, which are usually permanent, certifications and licenses are often conditional. They must be renewed. They can be suspended. They can be revoked. This creates a professional environment in which competence is not merely achieved once, but continually demonstrated.

This distinction matters—especially in an era of rapid technological change.

As automation and artificial intelligence reshape white-collar work, many roles built around abstraction, analysis, or information processing are becoming easier to replicate at scale. At the same time, professions grounded in physical presence, regulated responsibility, interpersonal judgment, or legal accountability remain resistant to full automation.

It is not that these jobs cannot be assisted by technology—they often are—but that they require a licensed human being to stand behind the outcome.

In this sense, certification and licensure are not barriers to entry. They are anchors of trust in a volatile labor market. They signal not just that someone knows something, but that they are accountable for what they do.

The professions in this book occupy a crucial middle ground: more structured than informal gig work, less abstract than credential-heavy corporate roles, and deeply embedded in real-world consequences.

They are not immune to change. But they are adaptable, localized, and human-scaled.

Understanding how certification and licensure

function is essential to understanding why these careers endure—and why they may become more valuable, not less, as technology advances.

The chapters that follow explore these systems in practice, one profession at a time.

Artificial Intelligence and the Uneven Cost of Progress

Technological change has always disrupted work. What makes artificial intelligence different is not speed alone, but asymmetry.

Previous waves of automation—mechanization, electrification, computing—tended to replace physical labor first. AI targets something else: clerical work, analysis, pattern recognition, and communication. In other words, many of the jobs that were once presented as "safe" alternatives to manual or technical labor.

Estimates vary, but large labor studies consistently suggest that tens of millions of jobs worldwide are likely to be significantly altered or eliminated over the next decade due to AI-driven automation. At the same time, new roles will be created—some technical, some managerial, some speculative.

The problem is not whether jobs will be created.

The problem is who will be able to access them.

New AI-era jobs overwhelmingly favor people who already possess advanced education, technical fluency, geographic mobility, or social capital. These jobs often require retraining while unemployed, relocation to distant corporate hubs, or the ability to continually navigate abstract, rapidly changing systems.

For the average worker, the equation looks different.

Many people cannot pause income for reskilling. Many cannot move to tech hubs. Many do not want careers spent supervising machines, optimizing prompts, or competing with systems that improve faster than human learning curves. AI does not eliminate work evenly—it compresses the middle.

Roles built around routine knowledge, standardized reports, customer service scripts, basic analysis, scheduling, and compliance are increasingly handled faster, cheaper, and at scale by machines. The remaining human roles often become more precarious, more monitored, or more demanding, even as pay stagnates. At the same time, work that is:

- Physically grounded,
- Locally regulated,
- Legally accountable,
- Dependent on human presence or judgment,

has proven to be far more resistant to full automation.

AI can assist a water treatment operator—but it cannot hold the license. AI can analyze inspection data—but it cannot legally certify a bridge. AI can recommend hearing aid settings—but it cannot be accountable to a patient or a state board. This distinction matters.

The challenge for most people is not "How do I compete with AI?" It is "How do I position myself where AI cannot replace me outright?"

The professions in this book occupy that position by design. They are embedded in physical systems, public safety, health, infrastructure, and regulated trust. They evolve alongside technology rather than being erased by it.

This book does not promise immunity from change. No honest book can. What it offers instead is durability—careers structured around accountability, certification, and human responsibility rather than the ability to comprehend abstract concepts alone.

For people navigating an uncertain labor future, durability matters more than novelty.

Choosing Intentionally in an Automated Age

By the time you reach the final pages of this book, one fact should be clear: the future of work is not disappearing—it is reorganizing.

Artificial intelligence will continue to change how value is created, measured, and rewarded. Some roles will vanish. Others will fracture into narrower tasks. New titles will emerge, often faster than systems can meaningfully regulate them. Through it all, uncertainty will remain a constant.

What does not disappear is the need for trust, accountability, and human presence.

The professions described in this book endure because they solve real problems in the physical world, under real constraints, with real consequences. They are governed by standards that cannot be automated away and responsibilities that must ultimately rest with a human being.

This does not make them glamorous. It makes them reliable.

The purpose of this book is not to prescribe a single solution, nor to argue that everyone should pursue the same path. It is to restore choice—to remind readers that careers can be built deliberately, without excessive debt, without constant reinvention, and without surrendering dignity to algorithms or abstract hierarchies.

Some readers will recognize a profession here and feel immediate clarity. Others will simply walk away with a broader sense of what is possible—and that, too, is a success.

The future will reward those who understand where human responsibility still matters.

The final chapter returns to this idea, not with predictions or prescriptions, but with a simple question: What kind of work do you want to be accountable for?

Everything else follows from there.

Chapter 1

Healthcare: Where Human Presence Still Matters

Healthcare is often portrayed as the industry most vulnerable to artificial intelligence. Diagnostic algorithms improve yearly. Imaging software outperforms human pattern recognition in controlled settings. Administrative tasks are already heavily automated.

And yet, at the point of care, medicine remains stubbornly human.

The professions in this section exist where technology meets the living body—and where abstraction breaks down. They involve unconscious patients, fragile physiology, invasive procedures, and outcomes that cannot be deferred or reversed. In these environments, machines assist, but people remain responsible.

Much of modern healthcare depends not on physicians alone, but on a wide network of technicians and technologists whose work rarely draws attention. These roles are frequently misunderstood as auxiliary or secondary. In reality, they form the operational backbone of diagnosis and treatment. Without them, advanced medicine simply does not function.

These professions also reveal an uncomfortable truth about automation: intelligence is not the same as accountability. When a patient is harmed, a diagnosis missed, or a treatment fails, society demands a human chain of responsibility. Licensure, certification, and regulation exist not to exclude, but to establish trust.

Importantly, many of these careers do not require medical school or four-year degrees. They rely instead on focused training, certification, and the ability to perform under pressure. They reward reliability, attention, and judgment more than academic pedigree. For those willing to master a narrow but critical skill set, they offer meaningful work and long-term stability.

The chapters that follow explore healthcare professions that operate quietly but decisively—often at night, often out of sight, and often at moments when patients are most vulnerable. They are not immune to technological change. But they are anchored in something automation cannot replace: The necessity of a trained human being, present when it matters most.

Profile 1

Board Certified Hearing Instrument Specialist (BCHIS)
Alternate Titles: Hearing Instrument Specialist (HIS), Hearing Aid Specialist

---

What This Profession Does

A Board Certified Hearing Instrument Specialist evaluates hearing loss, fits and programs hearing instruments, and provides ongoing patient care. The role focuses specifically on hearing aids and assistive listening devices rather than broad diagnostic audiology.

The work is intensely human. Patients often arrive frustrated, withdrawn, or anxious after years of diminished hearing. The specialist translates clinical measurements into practical improvement—restoring conversation, safety, and social connection. Follow-up care is central: hearing aids require adjustment, education, and trust over time.

Most BCHIS professionals work in clinics, private practices, or local hearing centers. Some operate independent practices serving defined communities.

Why This Career Survives AI

AI can analyze audiograms and suggest device settings. It cannot assume legal responsibility for patient outcomes.

Hearing care requires:

- In-person assessment and physical device fitting
- Interpretation of patient feedback and behavior
- Ethical responsibility for regulated medical devices
- State licensure and professional accountability AI functions as a tool. The licensed practitioner remains essential.

Entry Requirements

- High school diploma or GED
- Minimum age requirement (varies by state)
- Comfort with patient interaction, often with older adults
- Manual dexterity and attention to detail
- No college degree is required.

Training and Certification Path

Entry typically follows a structured sequence:

- State-approved training program (often online or hybrid)
- Supervised internship or apprenticeship (commonly 6–12 months)
- State licensing examination
- National Board Certification through the International Hearing Society (BCHIS)
- Total time to complete training is usually 12–24 months, depending on state regulations.

Licensing, Oversight, and Accountability

Hearing Instrument Specialists are regulated at the state level.
Oversight includes:

- Licensing boards
- Continuing education requirements
- Ethical standards and disciplinary authority

Licensure must be renewed. Certification requires ongoing education, keeping practitioners current as technology evolves.

Cost, Time, and Debt Reality

- Training programs: typically low four figures
- Apprenticeship: often paid or modestly compensated
- Exams and licensing fees: predictable and limited

Most practitioners enter the field without student loan debt.

Income and Work Stability

- Entry-level income is steady but modest
- Experienced practitioners earn solid middle-class incomes
- Independent or commission-based models may earn more

Demand is supported by an aging population and increased awareness of hearing health.

Who Tends to Thrive in This Role

This profession suits people who:

- Value one-on-one patient relationships
- Are patient, empathetic, and methodical
- Enjoy applied technology with real-world impact
- Prefer service and stability over prestige

Trade-Offs and Realities

- Some settings include sales expectations
- Work can involve repeated adjustments, maintenance, and follow-ups
- Emotional labor is real
- The work is not glamorous. It is consequential.

The Bigger Picture

A typical day includes hearing evaluations, device fittings, follow-up adjustments, patient education, cleaning and maintenance, and documentation. Success is measured quietly—when someone hears clearly again.

Getting Started

- Review your state's licensing requirements
- Explore state-approved training programs
- Visit the International Hearing Society for certification details
- Speak with practicing specialists about employment models

Profile 2

Ophthalmic Technician
Alternate Titles: Ophthalmic Assistant, Eye Care Technician

What This Profession Does

An Ophthalmic Technician supports ophthalmologists and optometrists by performing eye exams, operating diagnostic equipment, assisting with procedures, and preparing patients for care. The role combines technical accuracy with calm, professional patient interaction.

Technicians gather medical histories, measure visual acuity and eye pressure, conduct imaging, and ensure physicians receive accurate clinical data. Patients often arrive anxious or experiencing vision loss; steady reassurance is part of the job.

Most technicians work in ophthalmology clinics, medical offices, hospitals, or surgical centers.

Why This Career Survives AI

AI can assist with image analysis and screening. It cannot replace physical examinations, patient preparation, or supervised clinical care.

Ophthalmic Technicians provide:

- Hands-on testing and measurements
- Equipment operation requiring judgment and adjustment

- Direct patient management
- Accountability within regulated medical settings

AI enhances efficiency. It does not replace the technician.

Entry Requirements

- High school diploma or GED
- Comfort in medical environments
- Strong attention to detail and hand–eye coordination
- Professional communication skills

No college degree is required for entry-level roles.

Training and Certification Path

Common entry pathways include:

- On-the-job training in a clinical practice
- Short certificate programs (often 6–12 months)
- Professional certification is available through JCAHPO, including:
- Certified Ophthalmic Assistant (COA)
- Certified Ophthalmic Technician (COT)
- Certified Ophthalmic Medical Technologist (COMT)

Many employers support certification after hire.

Licensing, Oversight, and Accountability

Ophthalmic Technicians work under licensed physicians and within regulated healthcare systems.

Accountability includes:

- Clinical supervision
- Medical protocols and privacy compliance
- Certification standards and continuing education

Trust is enforced through healthcare regulation rather than independent licensure.

Cost, Time, and Debt Reality

- Entry via employer training: often no cost
- Certificate programs: low four figures
- Certification exams and materials: modest

Most technicians enter the field debt-free.

Income and Work Stability

- Entry-level pay is modest
- Certification and experience increase earning potential
- Demand is steady due to aging populations and chronic eye conditions

---

Who Tends to Thrive in This Role

This role suits people who:

- Enjoy structured medical environments
- Are calm, precise, and patient-focused
- Want clinical responsibility without medical school
- Value steady, meaningful work

Trade-Offs and Realities

- Repetitive procedures are common
- Some tasks are uncomfortable for patients
- Standing and close visual work are routine
- Consistency and focus matter.

The Bigger Picture

A typical day includes preparing exam rooms, conducting vision tests, operating imaging equipment, assisting physicians, documenting findings, and coordinating patient flow. The pace is busy but predictable.

Getting Started

- Apply to ophthalmology or eye-care practices offering training
- Review JCAHPO certification pathways
- Talk with technicians about advancement options

Profile 3

Sleep Technologist (Polysomnographic Technologist)

What This Profession Does.

Sleep Technologists diagnose and monitor sleep disorders by conducting overnight sleep studies—most commonly in hospital sleep labs or specialized clinics. While patients sleep, the technologist attaches and monitors an array of sensors that track brain waves (EEG), eye movement, muscle activity, heart rhythm, breathing patterns, oxygen saturation, and limb movement.

They are not passive observers. Throughout the night, Sleep Technologists actively troubleshoot equipment, adjust sensors, respond to breathing events, initiate therapeutic interventions such as CPAP titration, and ensure patient safety. After the study, they analyze raw physiological data and prepare detailed reports for interpretation by sleep physicians.

This is clinical work performed in real time, with real patients, under conditions that demand calm judgment, technical competence, and human reassurance—often at 2 a.m.

Why This Career Survives AI

Sleep medicine lives at the intersection of biology,

behavior, and human variability—an environment where automation struggles.

While AI can assist with scoring sleep data, it cannot:

- Prepare and position a living patient
- Detect subtle behavioral or physiological anomalies in real time
- Respond to anxiety, claustrophobia, or medical distress
- Make judgment calls during emergent breathing or cardiac events
- Ensure ethical, legal, and clinical chain-of-custody for diagnostic data

Sleep studies require hands-on presence, trust, and accountability. Patients are vulnerable, unconscious, and wired to medical equipment. That reality alone creates a durable human moat.

As long as humans sleep—and develop sleep disorders—this profession endures.

Training, Certification, and Entry Path

Unlike many healthcare careers, Sleep Technology offers multiple non-degree entry paths, depending on state and employer requirements.

Typical routes include:

- A certificate program (often 6–12 months)
- On-the-job training in a sleep lab
- An associate degree in polysomnography or allied health (optional, not universal)

Professional credentialing is commonly through:

- BRPT (Board of Registered Polysomnographic Technologists)
- RPSGT (Registered Polysomnographic Technologist)

Licensure requirements vary by state, but many allow employment prior to full credentialing.

This is a field where competence and certification matter more than formal academic pedigree.

Compensation and Stability

Sleep Technologists earn solid middle-class incomes, with variation by region, shift, and experience.

- Typical pay range: $50,000–$80,000+ annually
- Night shifts often pay premiums
- Hospitals, sleep labs, and clinics provide steady demand
- Aging populations and rising sleep disorder diagnoses support long-term stability

While not a path to sudden wealth, it offers reliable income, benefits, and employability—especially for those willing to work nights.

Who This Career Is For

This profession is well suited to individuals who:

- Prefer technical, structured work
- Are comfortable with patients but not drawn to bedside nursing
- Can remain alert and calm overnight

- Value certification over credentials and skills over titles
- Want a healthcare role without medical school or crushing debt

It is particularly attractive to career changers, veterans, and second-career adults seeking meaningful work with a clear on-ramp.

The Bigger Picture

Sleep Technologists occupy a quiet but essential niche in modern medicine. They are trusted stewards of unconscious patients, interpreters of invisible biological signals, and indispensable partners to physicians.

In an era obsessed with screens, algorithms, and speed, this profession reminds us of something enduring:

Some work can only be done by a human—present, alert, and responsible—while the rest of the world sleeps.

Profile 4

Neurodiagnostic Technologist (EEG Technologist)

What The Profession Does.

Neurodiagnostic Technologists perform tests that measure the electrical activity of the brain and nervous system. Their primary tool is the electroencephalogram (EEG), used to diagnose conditions such as epilepsy, brain injuries, tumors, sleep disorders, encephalopathy, and unexplained loss of consciousness.

In hospitals, clinics, and epilepsy monitoring units, these technologists prepare patients, apply electrodes using precise anatomical landmarks, operate sophisticated diagnostic equipment, and monitor brain activity in real time. They must recognize abnormal waveforms, seizure activity, and emergent neurological events as they occur.

This is not a passive recording role. Neurodiagnostic Technologists actively intervene—alerting physicians, extending studies, initiating protocols, and ensuring patient safety during seizures or other critical events.

They work close to the raw signals of the human brain.

Why This Career Survives AI

While AI can assist with pattern recognition, neurodiagnostics depends on context, judgment, and responsibility—all areas where automation remains brittle.

AI cannot:

- Prepare and position patients accurately
- Manage seizures, confusion, or panic during testing
- Adjust electrode placement in response to real-time signal artifacts
- Distinguish clinically relevant abnormalities from movement, medication, or behavioral effects
- Assume legal and ethical responsibility for neurological monitoring

EEGs are noisy, human, and situational. Artifacts from blinking, movement, sweat, anxiety, or medication can mimic pathology. Determining what matters requires trained human discernment, not just signal processing.

As long as brains malfunction in unpredictable ways, this profession remains essential.

Training, Certification, and Entry Path

Neurodiagnostic Technology offers multiple entry routes that do not require a four-year degree, though formal training is common.

Typical paths include:

- Certificate programs (often 12–24 months)
- Associate degrees in neurodiagnostic technology or allied health
- Structured hospital-based training programs

Professional certification is typically through:

- ABRET (American Board of Registration of Electroencephalographic and Evoked Potential Technologists)

- R. EEG T. (Registered EEG Technologist)

Some states require licensure; many do not. In most cases, employment is possible prior to full certification, with credentials earned on the job.

As with other hidden professions, certification and demonstrated competence outweigh academic prestige.

Compensation and Stability

Neurodiagnostic Technologists earn dependable, above-average incomes, especially with experience or specialization.

- Typical pay range: $55,000–$85,000+ annually
- Higher pay in hospitals, epilepsy units, and travel positions
- On-call, weekend, and specialty studies increase earnings
- Strong demand driven by aging populations and neurological disease prevalence

This is a career with portable skills, national credentialing, and long-term relevance.

Who This Career Is For

This profession suits individuals who:

- Are detail-oriented and methodical
- Can remain calm during medical emergencies
- Are fascinated by neuroscience without pursuing medical school
- Prefer technical mastery over managerial ambition
- Want meaningful clinical work without extreme educational debt.

It is particularly well suited to career changers, veterans, and analytically minded individuals seeking purpose-driven healthcare roles.

The Bigger Picture

Neurodiagnostic Technologists work at the boundary between consciousness and malfunction—where machines alone are not enough, and human presence matters.

In an era that promises brain-computer interfaces and algorithmic medicine, this profession quietly proves a deeper truth:

Understanding the human brain still requires a human in the room.

Profile 5

Dialysis Technician (Patient Care Technician – Dialysis)

What The Profession Does.

Dialysis Technicians operate and monitor life-sustaining equipment for patients whose kidneys can no longer function adequately on their own. In outpatient dialysis centers and hospitals, they prepare dialysis machines, insert and monitor needles, measure vital signs, administer treatments under clinical protocols, and observe patients for complications during sessions that often last several hours.

They work directly with chronically ill patients—many of whom require dialysis multiple times per week for years. Technicians must recognize warning signs such as sudden blood pressure changes, clotting, infection, or machine malfunction and respond immediately.

This is not auxiliary work. For patients with end-stage renal disease, dialysis technicians are part of the thin line between stability and medical crisis.

Why This Career Survives AI

Dialysis is continuous, invasive, and high-risk, requiring constant human oversight.

AI cannot:

- Cannulate vascular access safely and consistently
- Respond to patient distress, pain, or sudden physiological changes
- Detect subtle human cues of impending complications
- Take legal and ethical responsibility for life-support procedures
- Build the trust required for long-term, repetitive care.

While machines perform the filtration, humans ensure survival. Dialysis is a setting where failure is immediate and consequences are severe—conditions that favor trained professionals over automation.

This is work that demands presence, judgment, and accountability.

Training, Certification, and Entry Path

Dialysis Technician roles are among the most accessible in clinical medicine.

Typical requirements include:

- High school diploma or GED
- Employer-provided training (often 3–6 months)
- Certification within a defined period after hire

Common credentials include:

- CCHT (Certified Clinical Hemodialysis Technician)
- CCHT-A (Advanced)
- CDT (Certified Dialysis Technician)

Federal regulations require certification within a specific timeframe, but formal college degrees are usually not required.

This is a true earn-while-you-learn profession.

Compensation and Stability

Dialysis Technicians earn modest but reliable incomes, with strong job security.

- Typical pay range: $40,000–$60,000+ annually
- Overtime and shift differentials common
- Large national providers offer benefits and advancement paths
- Chronic kidney disease prevalence ensures steady demand

While not high-paying at entry level, this role offers remarkable employment stability and opportunities to move into nursing, administration, or clinical specialization.

Who This Career Is For

This profession is well suited to individuals who:

- Are comfortable with medical procedures and bodily fluids
- Value meaningful, patient-centered work
- Can maintain focus during repetitive, high-stakes tasks
- Want a clinical healthcare role without long

academic pipelines

- Prefer job security over prestige

It is particularly appropriate for those seeking immediate employability in healthcare.

The Bigger Picture

Dialysis Technicians work quietly at the infrastructure level of modern medicine—keeping thousands of people alive every day, one treatment at a time.

In debates about automation and efficiency, this profession underscores a reality that is easy to overlook:

Life-support systems do not run themselves.

Profile 6

Respiratory Therapy Assistant (Respiratory Care Technician / Pulmonary Assistant — title varies by employer)

What The Profession Does

Respiratory Therapy Assistants support licensed Respiratory Therapists in delivering care to patients with breathing disorders, lung disease, and compromised airways. They work in hospitals, long-term care facilities, rehabilitation centers, and outpatient pulmonary clinics.

Their responsibilities include preparing and maintaining respiratory equipment, administering prescribed breathing treatments, monitoring oxygen delivery systems, assisting during ventilator care, performing pulmonary function tests, and closely observing patients for signs of respiratory distress.

Breathing is not optional. When it falters, seconds matter—and these assistants are often the first to notice subtle changes that precede a crisis.

Why This Career Survives AI

Respiratory care exists in a domain where automation assists but cannot replace human presence.

AI cannot:

- Properly position masks, tubing, and airway

devices on living patients

- Calm frightened or panicking individuals struggling to breathe
- Adjust treatment delivery in response to real-time patient behavior
- Recognize non-numeric cues such as anxiety, fatigue, or confusion
- Accept responsibility during respiratory emergencies.

Ventilators, oxygen concentrators, and monitoring systems are powerful tools—but they are only as safe as the humans supervising them.

Respiratory care remains fundamentally physical, immediate, and high-risk—conditions under which automation remains subordinate.

Training, Certification, and Entry Path

Respiratory Therapy Assistant roles typically do not require a four-year degree and often serve as entry points into respiratory care.

Common pathways include:

- On-the-job training under licensed Respiratory Therapists
- Certificate programs in respiratory or pulmonary care
- Allied health or clinical assistant training programs.

Certification requirements vary by state and employer. Some roles require:

- Basic Life Support (BLS)
- CPR certification

- Employer-specific respiratory competencies

This field prioritizes demonstrated skill, reliability, and clinical awareness over academic pedigree.

Compensation and Stability

Respiratory Therapy Assistants earn steady incomes with strong employment stability.

- Typical pay range: $40,000–$60,000+ annually
- Hospital and night shifts often pay premiums
- High demand in aging populations and post-acute care settings
- Pandemic-era awareness permanently increased staffing needs.

While not the highest-paid role in respiratory medicine, it offers consistent work, benefits, and clear advancement paths.

Who This Career Is For

This profession is well suited to individuals who:

- Want hands-on clinical work without long educational commitments
- Can stay calm during breathing emergencies
- Prefer structured, protocol-driven environments
- Are comfortable working closely with patients and equipment
- May wish to advance later into licensed respiratory therapy

It is an especially strong option for those seeking fast entry into healthcare with real responsibility.

The Bigger Picture

Respiratory Therapy Assistants operate at the most fundamental boundary of medicine: air in, air out.

In discussions about AI-driven healthcare, this role illustrates a truth that no algorithm escapes:

When breathing fails, someone must be physically present to intervene.

Profile 7

Pulmonary Function Technologist (PFT Technologist)

What The Profession Does.

Pulmonary Function Technologists conduct specialized diagnostic tests that measure how well a patient's lungs work. These tests evaluate airflow, lung volume, gas exchange, and respiratory muscle strength and are essential in diagnosing asthma, chronic obstructive pulmonary disease (COPD), pulmonary fibrosis, occupational lung disease, and pre-operative surgical risk.

In hospitals, pulmonary clinics, and cardiopulmonary labs, PFT Technologists coach patients through a series of precise breathing maneuvers while operating sensitive diagnostic equipment. The accuracy of each test depends not only on machinery, but on the technologist's ability to instruct, motivate, and judge patient effort in real time.

Poor coaching produces bad data. Good technologists produce reliable diagnoses.

Why This Career Survives AI

Pulmonary testing depends on human cooperation and real-time judgment—conditions that resist full automation.

AI cannot:

- Coach patients through complex breathing instructions
- Assess whether a patient's effort is valid or compromised
- Adjust testing protocols on the fly
- Recognize behavioral, physical, or cognitive barriers affecting results
- Take responsibility for diagnostic integrity.

Machines record airflow; humans determine whether the data mean anything. Subtle lapses in effort, misunderstanding, anxiety, or fatigue can invalidate results, and recognizing those failures requires a trained human in the room.

As long as diagnosis depends on patient behavior, this role remains human-anchored.

Training, Certification, and Entry Path

Pulmonary Function Technology typically requires targeted training rather than extensive degrees.

Common entry routes include:

- On-the-job training within cardiopulmonary departments
- Certificate programs in pulmonary diagnostics
- Backgrounds as respiratory therapy assistants or related allied health roles.

Professional credentials may include:

- CPFT (Certified Pulmonary Function Technologist)
- RPFT (Registered Pulmonary Function

Technologist).

Certification is often employer-preferred rather than mandatory, and advancement occurs through demonstrated competence rather than formal academic progression.

Compensation and Stability

Pulmonary Function Technologists earn solid, stable incomes with predictable schedules.

- Typical pay range: $50,000–$75,000+ annually
- Daytime hours common compared to other respiratory roles
- Growing demand due to aging populations and chronic lung disease
- Strong relevance in pre-operative and occupational health settings

This role offers a rare balance of technical depth, patient interaction, and work-life stability.

Who This Career Is For

This profession is well suited to individuals who:

- Enjoy precision, coaching, and problem-solving
- Prefer diagnostic work over acute crisis response
- Are comfortable working one-on-one with patients
- Value technical mastery without prolonged education

- Want healthcare work with predictable hours

It is especially attractive to mid-career entrants and clinicians seeking less shift-based work.

The Bigger Picture

Pulmonary Function Technologists reveal a quiet truth about modern medicine:

Data does not speak for itself.

In a world increasingly obsessed with sensors and algorithms, this profession survives because diagnosis still depends on human guidance, judgment, and accountability.

Why Life-Critical Healthcare Resists Automation

The first professions in this book share a common trait that is easy to miss in debates about artificial intelligence: they operate where failure is immediate and consequences are personal.

Sleep Technologists, Neurodiagnostic Technologists, Dialysis Technicians, Respiratory Assistants, and Pulmonary Function Technologists all work in environments where machines assist—but humans remain responsible. Sensors record. Software analyzes. Algorithms suggest. But when a patient stops breathing, seizes, panics, or deteriorates, someone must be physically present, trained, and accountable.

Automation excels at repetition and pattern recognition. It struggles with ambiguity, context, and human variability. Healthcare, especially at the diagnostic and life-support level, is saturated with all three.

A sleep study is not just data collection; it is the management of an unconscious human being. An EEG is not a clean signal; it is a noisy mixture of biology, behavior, anxiety, medication, and chance. Dialysis is not a procedure that can be "set and forget"; it is a sustained intervention where small deviations can become medical emergencies. Pulmonary testing depends as much on coaching and judgment as it does on equipment.

In each case, technology extends human capability—but does not replace human responsibility.

This distinction matters. Much of the public

conversation about AI assumes that if a task can be partially automated, it can be fully automated. That assumption collapses in environments where trust, ethics, and liability dominate. When a patient is harmed, there must be a human chain of responsibility. Machines do not hold licenses. Algorithms do not testify. Software does not comfort frightened patients at three in the morning.

These professions also expose another blind spot in the automation narrative: credential inflation. None of these roles require medical school. Few require four-year degrees. What they require instead is certification, competence, and the ability to perform under pressure. They are not "low skill" jobs; they are narrowly skilled, deeply consequential ones.

For workers navigating an uncertain economic future, this matters. Life-critical healthcare roles offer a form of security that does not depend on prestige, pedigree, or constant reinvention. They depend on something older and more durable: the continued fragility of the human body.

As long as humans breathe, sleep, seize, and fail in unpredictable ways, these professions will endure. Artificial intelligence may change how the work is done—but not the need for someone to do it.

The chapters that follow move beyond healthcare into other sectors where the same pattern holds. Different tools. Different environments. The same underlying truth: Where failure carries real-world consequences, humans remain indispensable.

Chapter 2

Infrastructure: The Work That Holds Society Together

Modern society runs on systems most people never see and rarely think about—until they fail.

Clean water arrives without ceremony. Electricity hums behind walls. Waste disappears. Roads remain passable. Buildings stand. Signals transmit. These are not conveniences; they are the conditions of civilization. When they break, daily life unravels quickly and without mercy.

Infrastructure work is often described as technical, mechanical, or routine. In reality, it is custodial. These professions do not innovate in public view; they maintain continuity. They keep yesterday's systems functioning today, and today's systems functioning tomorrow. The success of the work is measured by invisibility.

This makes infrastructure labor easy to undervalue—and hard to automate.

Automation performs best in environments that are clean, predictable, and fully specified. Infrastructure exists in none of those. Pipes age. Grids strain.

Weather intrudes. Materials degrade. Human behavior remains inconsistent. Every system is a patchwork of legacy decisions layered over decades, sometimes centuries.

When something goes wrong, there is no clean reset. There is only diagnosis, judgment, and intervention under imperfect conditions—often in the dark, in the cold, or under time pressure.

Artificial intelligence can assist with forecasting, monitoring, and optimization. It can flag anomalies and suggest responses. What it cannot do is take responsibility for physical systems embedded in the real world. It cannot climb a pole during a storm, enter a confined space, or decide which failure must be addressed first when multiple systems degrade at once.

Infrastructure professions are also governed by trust. Water operators safeguard public health. Lineworkers protect communities from fire and electrocution. Inspectors determine whether buildings are safe to occupy. These roles exist inside regulatory, legal, and ethical frameworks that require human accountability.

Like life-critical healthcare, infrastructure work resists automation not because it is simple—but because it is too consequential.

These professions rarely require elite degrees. Many rely on apprenticeships, certification, and long experience. They reward reliability over ambition and competence over credentials. They offer something increasingly rare in modern labor markets: durable usefulness.

As societies age, urbanize, and confront climate stress, the demand for people who can maintain and repair physical systems only increases. Infrastructure does not scale like software. It must be touched, inspected, repaired, and rebuilt—again and again.

The following profiles explore careers that operate beneath the surface of daily life. They are not glamorous. They are not optional. And when they disappear, everything else follows.

Profile 8

Water Treatment Plant Operator

What The Profession Does.

Water Treatment Plant Operators are responsible for producing safe, potable drinking water for entire communities. Working in municipal or regional treatment facilities, they oversee the processes that remove contaminants, neutralize pathogens, adjust chemical balances, and ensure water meets strict public health standards before it enters the distribution system.

Their daily work includes monitoring treatment systems, adjusting chemical dosages, interpreting sensor data, conducting laboratory tests, maintaining equipment, and responding to system alarms or irregularities. Operators must understand how raw water quality changes with weather, runoff, seasonal variation, and infrastructure age—and how those changes affect treatment decisions.

When water leaves the plant, millions of people trust that it is safe. That trust rests largely on the judgment of a small number of operators.

Why This Career Survives AI

Water treatment is too critical to fully automate.

AI can assist with monitoring and optimization, but it cannot:

- Take legal responsibility for public health

outcomes
- Make judgment calls during ambiguous or cascading system failures
- Respond creatively to unexpected contamination events
- Perform physical inspections, repairs, and emergency interventions
- Balance competing risks when data is incomplete or contradictory

Water systems are complex, aging, and deeply contextual. A sensor can fail. A reading can be misleading. Weather can change conditions faster than models anticipate. When something looks wrong, a human operator must decide whether to shut down, divert, dose differently, or escalate—often under time pressure.

When drinking water is compromised, consequences are immediate, political, and severe. For that reason alone, humans remain firmly in the loop.

Training, Certification, and Entry Path

Water Treatment Plant Operator roles are among the most accessible careers in infrastructure.

Typical requirements include:
- High school diploma or GED
- On-the-job training or apprenticeship
- State-issued certification tied to system size and complexity.

Certification is usually tiered (Grade I–IV or similar), allowing operators to:
- Enter the field at a basic level

- Advance through experience and examination
- Increase responsibility and compensation over time.

Formal college degrees are often optional. What matters is licensure, competence, and trustworthiness.

This is a profession built on gradual mastery rather than academic escalation.

Compensation and Stability

Water Treatment Plant Operators earn solid, reliable incomes with exceptional job security.

- Typical pay range: $50,000–$90,000+ annually
- Higher grades and supervisory roles earn more
- Municipal employment often includes strong benefits and pensions
- Demand is stable and recession-resistant.

People can delay many purchases. They cannot stop drinking water.

Who This Career Is For

This profession is well suited to individuals who:

- Prefer responsibility over recognition
- Are comfortable with technical systems and regulatory standards
- Can work independently and make careful decisions.

- Value long-term stability and public service
- Want meaningful work without credential inflation

It is especially attractive to those seeking quiet authority rather than public-facing roles.

The Bigger Picture

Water Treatment Plant Operators sit at one of the most fundamental choke points of modern life. When they succeed, nothing happens. When they fail, everything does.

In an age fascinated by digital disruption, this profession offers a reminder that some systems are not optional, not scalable, and not safely delegated to algorithms.

Civilization begins with clean water—and someone must ensure it stays that way.

Profile 9

Electrical Lineworker (Power Line Technician)

What The Profession Does.

Electrical Lineworkers build, maintain, and repair the systems that transmit electrical power from generation facilities to homes, hospitals, businesses, and critical infrastructure. They install and service overhead and underground power lines, transformers, substations, and related equipment—often under hazardous conditions.

Lineworkers respond to outages caused by storms, accidents, equipment failure, and natural disasters. They work at height, in confined spaces, around high-voltage systems that can kill instantly if mishandled. Precision, situational awareness, and strict adherence to safety protocols are non-negotiable.

When the power goes out, lineworkers restore it—frequently at night, in extreme weather, and under intense public pressure.

Why This Career Survives AI

Electrical linework exists in the physical world under dangerous, unpredictable conditions—an environment where full automation remains impractical.

AI cannot:

- Safely climb poles or enter unstable environments
- Perform delicate physical work around live high-voltage systems
- Adapt to damaged infrastructure that deviates from schematics
- Make real-time safety judgments when conditions change
- Accept responsibility for life-and-death decisions.

Power grids are aging, customized, and often poorly documented. Storm damage rarely matches models. Every repair is a judgment call involving weather, load, crew safety, and downstream consequences.

When mistakes can kill workers or start fires, humans remain indispensable.

Training, Certification, and Entry Path

Electrical Linework relies on apprenticeship, not academic pedigree.

Typical entry includes:

- High school diploma or GED
- Apprenticeship programs (often 3–4 years)
- Classroom instruction combined with paid field training.

Requirements commonly include:

- Commercial driver's license (CDL)
- Safety certifications
- Utility or union qualifications

Formal college degrees are not required. Advancement is based on experience, demonstrated competence, and safety record.

Compensation and Stability

Electrical Lineworkers are among the best-paid skilled infrastructure professionals.

- Typical pay range: $70,000–$120,000+ annually
- Significant overtime during outages and emergencies
- Strong union representation in many regions
- Excellent benefits and retirement plans.

Demand is persistent and growing as grids age, populations expand, and climate-driven weather events increase.

Who This Career Is For

This profession is well suited to individuals who:

- Are physically capable and safety-focused
- Can work under pressure and in dangerous conditions
- Prefer tangible results over office work
- Value teamwork, discipline, and responsibility
- Want high pay without credential inflation

It is not for everyone—but for the right person, it offers respect, purpose, and economic security.

The Bigger Picture

Electrical Lineworkers maintain one of the most fragile achievements of modern civilization: continuous power. When electricity disappears, everything else falters—communication, healthcare, water, finance, and transportation.

In conversations about automation and efficiency, this profession stands as a reminder:

Someone still has to climb the pole.

Profile 10

Power Plant Operator

What The Profession Does.

Power Plant Operators control the systems that generate electricity for regional and national grids. Working in fossil fuel, nuclear, hydroelectric, and renewable energy facilities, they monitor and regulate turbines, boilers, reactors, generators, and control systems to ensure continuous, stable power production.

From centralized control rooms, operators adjust output, manage load changes, respond to alarms, and coordinate with grid operators to balance supply and demand. They conduct equipment checks, follow strict operating procedures, and intervene during abnormal conditions to prevent equipment damage, environmental harm, or catastrophic failure.

Unlike many technical roles, power plant operation is continuous. Plants run 24 hours a day. Operators work rotating shifts, nights, weekends, and holidays—because electricity does not pause.

Why This Career Survives AI

Power generation is too dangerous and too consequential to operate without human oversight.

AI can assist with forecasting, optimization, and

anomaly detection, but it cannot:

- Assume legal and regulatory responsibility for plant operations
- Manage cascading failures under novel conditions
- Balance competing risks when procedures conflict with real-world conditions
- Coordinate human teams during emergencies
- Exercise judgment when data is incomplete or contradictory.

Power plants are complex, tightly coupled systems where small errors can escalate rapidly. When alarms trigger, someone must decide what matters, what can wait, and what requires immediate shutdown.

When the cost of failure includes blackouts, environmental damage, or loss of life, humans remain firmly in control.

Training, Certification, and Entry Path

Power Plant Operators typically enter through structured training rather than formal degrees.

Common pathways include:

- On-the-job training at generation facilities
- Apprenticeship-style progression through operator levels
- Military or industrial operations backgrounds.

Licensing and certification depend on plant type:

- Fossil fuel and hydro plants rely on internal qualification systems
- Nuclear operators require rigorous federal

licensing
- Renewable facilities maintain plant-specific credentials

Four-year degrees are often optional. What matters is procedural discipline, situational awareness, and trust.

Compensation and Stability

Power Plant Operators earn strong incomes with exceptional job security.

- Typical pay range: $70,000–$120,000+ annually
- Higher compensation for nuclear and senior operators
- Shift differentials and overtime common
- Long-term demand as aging plants retire and new generation comes online

Electric grids cannot be outsourced or fully automated.

Who This Career Is For

This profession is well suited to individuals who:
- Are comfortable with responsibility and high-stakes decision-making
- Can work rotating shifts without complaint
- Prefer systems thinking over physical labor
- Follow procedures meticulously while remaining adaptable
- Value stability, respect, and long-term

employment.

It rewards discipline over charisma and competence over credentials.

The Bigger Picture

Power Plant Operators sit at the starting point of nearly every modern system. Hospitals, water treatment plants, communications networks, and financial systems all depend on uninterrupted power generation.

In discussions about smart grids and autonomous systems, this profession anchors reality:

Someone must remain awake in the control room.

Profile 11

Substation Technician

What They Do

Substation Technicians install, maintain, test, and repair the electrical substations that regulate voltage as power moves from generation facilities to transmission and distribution networks. Substations step electricity up for long-distance transmission and back down for safe delivery to cities, industries, and homes.

Working in high-voltage environments, technicians service transformers, breakers, relays, and control systems. They perform inspections, run diagnostic tests, calibrate protective equipment, and respond to failures that could otherwise cascade into regional outages.

Substations are not visible to the public, but they are where grid stability is either preserved—or lost.

Why This Career Survives AI

Substations are complex, customized, and dangerous physical environments.

AI can assist with monitoring and predictive maintenance, but it cannot:

- Safely work in live high-voltage yards
- Perform physical repairs or replacements
- Interpret ambiguous fault conditions in the

field
- Coordinate lockout/tagout procedures with crews
- Accept responsibility for grid protection decisions

Electrical infrastructure is not uniform. Many substations contain decades-old equipment, undocumented modifications, and site-specific quirks. When protective systems misbehave, human judgment prevents catastrophic failure.

This work exists at the intersection of precision and danger—an area where automation remains limited.

Training, Certification, and Entry Path

Substation Technicians typically enter through apprenticeships or utility training programs.

Common requirements include:
- High school diploma or GED
- Technical training or utility apprenticeship
- Safety and electrical certifications

Some technicians come from:
- Electrical linework
- Industrial electrical maintenance
- Military or power generation backgrounds

Formal four-year degrees are rarely required. Advancement is based on experience, reliability, and safety performance.

Compensation and Stability

Substation Technicians earn strong incomes and enjoy long-term job security.

- Typical pay range: $70,000–$110,000+ annually
- Overtime during outages and upgrades
- Strong benefits through utilities and unions
- Growing demand as grid modernization accelerates

Power systems cannot be maintained remotely.

Who This Career Is For

This profession is well suited to individuals who:

- Are meticulous and safety-focused
- Prefer technical precision over physical endurance
- Can work independently and as part of a crew
- Are comfortable with high responsibility
- Want infrastructure work without constant emergency response.

It rewards patience, discipline, and technical mastery.

The Bigger Picture

Substation Technicians work in the grid's quiet middle ground—rarely noticed, always essential. When substations fail, entire regions go dark. When they succeed, nothing happens.

In conversations about smart grids and automation, this role underscores a central truth:

The electrical grid is physical—and someone must keep it that way.

Profile 12

Elevator Mechanic

What The Profession Does.

Elevator Mechanics install, maintain, repair, and modernize elevators, escalators, moving walkways, and related lift systems. They work in residential buildings, hospitals, office towers, factories, transit hubs, and anywhere people or goods must move vertically or horizontally in confined spaces.

Their work includes assembling mechanical components, wiring electrical control systems, programming controllers, aligning rails, inspecting safety mechanisms, and troubleshooting failures. Maintenance and repair often occur in tight shafts, machine rooms, or above occupied spaces—frequently while buildings remain in use.

When an elevator fails, the consequences range from inconvenience to medical emergency. In high-rise cities, elevators are not amenities. They are core infrastructure.

Why This Career Survives AI

Elevator systems operate in unique, enclosed, high-risk physical environments where automation remains limited.

AI cannot:

- Safely enter shafts or machine rooms to perform repairs
- Physically align rails, doors, brakes, and counterweights
- Rescue trapped passengers during failures
- Adapt to older, customized, or partially undocumented systems
- Accept legal responsibility for life-safety equipment.

Elevators are governed by strict safety codes because failure can kill. Inspection, maintenance, and repair require licensed humans whose judgment carries legal and ethical weight.

As buildings grow taller and denser, the need for skilled human oversight increases, not decreases.

Training, Certification, and Entry Path

Elevator Mechanics typically enter the field through formal apprenticeships, not academic programs.

Common requirements include:

- High school diploma or GED
- Competitive apprenticeship (often 4–5 years)
- Classroom instruction combined with paid field training

Training covers:

- Mechanical systems
- Electrical theory
- Hydraulics

- Electronics and controls
- Safety codes and regulations

Most Elevator Mechanics are union members, and four-year college degrees are not required. Advancement depends on skill, safety record, and experience.

Compensation and Stability

Elevator Mechanics are among the highest-paid skilled trades.

- Typical pay range: $80,000–$130,000+ annually
- Strong union wages and benefits
- Overtime and emergency work common
- Exceptional long-term job security

Elevators cannot be outsourced, digitized, or maintained remotely.

Who This Career Is For

This profession is well suited to individuals who:

- Are mechanically inclined and detail-oriented
- Are comfortable working in confined or elevated spaces
- Take safety and responsibility seriously
- Prefer hands-on problem solving
- Want high income without credential inflation.

It is demanding, selective, and physically real—but deeply respected.

The Bigger Picture

Elevator Mechanics make vertical cities possible. Hospitals, high-rises, and dense urban life depend on their work functioning flawlessly, day after day.

In discussions about smart buildings and automation, this profession stands as a quiet rebuttal:

Gravity has not been automated away.

Profile 13

Building Inspector

What The Profession Does.

Building Inspectors ensure that structures are constructed, altered, and maintained in compliance with building codes, safety regulations, and zoning requirements. Working for municipalities or private inspection agencies, they examine residential, commercial, and industrial buildings at various stages of construction and occupancy.

Their inspections cover structural integrity, electrical systems, plumbing, fire safety, accessibility, and energy compliance. Inspectors review plans, conduct on-site evaluations, document deficiencies, and require corrections before projects can proceed or be occupied.

When a building is declared safe, the public assumes that someone competent has verified that claim. That assumption rests on the judgment of a building inspector.

Why This Career Survives AI

Building inspection is contextual, physical, and legally consequential.

AI can assist with plan review, checklists, and documentation, but it cannot:

- Perform comprehensive on-site inspections
- Interpret code intent under ambiguous conditions
- Judge workmanship quality in real-world environments
- Negotiate corrections with contractors and property owners
- Assume legal responsibility for safety determinations.

Codes are complex, evolving, and subject to interpretation. Buildings are not built in laboratory conditions. Inspectors must weigh risk, intent, and practicality—often under time pressure and political pressure.

When failures occur, inspectors—not software—are held accountable.

Training, Certification, and Entry Path

Building Inspectors typically enter the profession through experience-based pathways.

Common routes include:

- Backgrounds in construction trades (electrical, plumbing, carpentry)
- Technical or vocational training
- On-the-job training with municipal departments

Certification is usually required and may include:

- ICC (International Code Council) certifications
- State or local licensure

Formal four-year degrees are often optional. Advancement depends on certification breadth, field experience, and judgment.

Compensation and Stability

Building Inspectors earn solid, stable incomes with predictable schedules.

- Typical pay range: $60,000–$90,000+ annually
- Municipal benefits often strong
- Daytime hours common
- Demand tied to construction cycles but persistent over time

While not emergency work, it is high-responsibility work.

Who This Career Is For

This profession is well suited to individuals who:

- Understand construction and building systems
- Are comfortable enforcing standards
- Can communicate clearly and professionally
- Value public safety and accountability
- Prefer steady, structured work

It suits those who want authority without drama and responsibility without spectacle.

The Bigger Picture

Building Inspectors stand at a quiet checkpoint between private ambition and public safety. They are rarely thanked and often resisted—but their work prevents tragedies that never make headlines.

In debates about automation and efficiency, this profession reinforces a central theme:

Trust still requires a human signature.

Profile 14

Survey Technician

What The Profession Does.

Survey Technicians assist in measuring, mapping, and documenting land boundaries, elevations, and physical features used for construction, infrastructure, property ownership, and legal records. Working under licensed surveyors, they collect field data that determines where roads are built, utilities are placed, buildings are erected, and property lines are enforced.

Their work includes operating surveying instruments, GPS equipment, and data collectors; setting and locating boundary markers; recording measurements; and verifying that construction aligns with approved plans. Survey data becomes part of the legal and engineering record—errors can have lasting consequences.

Before anything is built, someone must determine where it belongs.

Why This Career Survives AI

Surveying is physical, situational, and legally binding—a combination that resists full automation.

AI can assist with data processing and mapping, but it cannot:

- Verify physical boundary markers in the field
- Resolve conflicts between historical records and real-world conditions
- Adapt to terrain, obstructions, and access limitations
- Exercise legal judgment when boundaries are disputed
- Accept responsibility for survey accuracy.

Land is irregular. Records are imperfect. Markers move, disappear, or were placed incorrectly decades ago. When inconsistencies arise, human judgment in the field resolves them.

Survey errors do not vanish. They compound.

Training, Certification, and Entry Path

Survey Technician roles offer accessible entry into a licensed profession.

Common pathways include:

- On-the-job training with surveying firms or agencies
- Certificate or associate degree programs in surveying or geomatics
- Technical training combined with field experience.

Licensure applies to surveyors, not technicians, but technicians advance through:

- Experience
- Certification (where applicable)
- Progressive responsibility.

Four-year degrees are typically optional at the technician level. Skill, reliability, and precision matter most.

Compensation and Stability

Survey Technicians earn steady incomes with long-term demand.

- Typical pay range: $45,000–$75,000+ annually
- Higher pay with experience or specialized projects
- Work spans public and private sectors
- Demand persists with construction, infrastructure renewal, and land management.

Disputes over land do not disappear with technology.

Who This Career Is For

This profession is well suited to individuals who:

- Enjoy outdoor and field-based work
- Are detail-oriented and methodical
- Can translate physical space into data
- Prefer tangible outcomes over abstraction
- Value accuracy and accountability.

It appeals to those who want a technical role without constant crisis.

The Bigger Picture

Survey Technicians work at the boundary between maps and reality. Their measurements determine ownership, access, and compliance—long after the instruments are packed away.

In conversations about automation and digital twins, this profession reminds us:

The ground still has the final say.

Why Infrastructure Resists Automation

Infrastructure is where abstraction ends.

Unlike software or digital services, infrastructure exists in the physical world—subject to gravity, corrosion, weather, wear, and human error. Water must flow. Power must remain synchronized. Buildings must stand. Trains must not collide. Fires must be detected in time. When these systems fail, the consequences are immediate and widely shared.

The professions in this section operate inside that reality.

Water and wastewater operators safeguard public health at a scale most people never consider. Electrical lineworkers, substation technicians, and power plant operators maintain systems that cannot be paused or restarted without consequence. Elevator mechanics make dense cities livable. Building inspectors enforce trust where private incentives often conflict with public safety. Survey technicians establish the physical and legal groundwork on which everything else depends. Railroad signal technicians prevent disasters through systems designed to fail conservatively rather than efficiently. Fire protection technicians ensure that life-safety systems function only once—but must function perfectly.

These are not legacy jobs waiting to be disrupted. They are constraint-heavy professions, shaped by regulation, liability, and physics.

Artificial intelligence performs best where systems are clean, predictable, and fully observable. Infrastructure systems are none of those. They are layered, aging, and often poorly documented. They operate under changing loads, extreme weather, and real-world damage. Sensors fail. Models drift. Data arrives late or incomplete.

When something goes wrong, there is no "undo."

AI can optimize, monitor, and assist. It can flag anomalies and suggest responses. But it cannot climb a pole in a storm, enter a confined space, restore power safely, certify a building, resolve a boundary dispute, or sign off on a life-safety system. It cannot assume legal responsibility when public systems fail.

That responsibility remains human by design.

Infrastructure also exposes a flaw in how modern labor is valued. Many of these professions require no four-year degree. Some require only a high school diploma, certification, and time. Yet they carry consequences far greater than many credential-heavy roles. They reward competence, reliability, and judgment—not pedigree.

They also offer something increasingly rare: durable necessity. Societies can delay upgrades, postpone innovation, and argue about policy. They cannot stop producing drinking water, using electricity, occupying buildings, or moving goods and people. Infrastructure must be maintained continuously, regardless of economic cycle or technological trend.

This is why these careers persist. Not because they resist change—but because they absorb it. New tools are integrated. New standards emerge. The work evolves. But the need for accountable humans in the loop remains.

As artificial intelligence advances, the most secure work will not be the most abstract. It will be the work anchored to the physical world, governed by trust, and constrained by reality.

Infrastructure does not scale like software. It must

be touched.

And someone must be willing to take responsibility when it breaks.

Chapter 3

MUNICIPAL CAREERS: THE PROFESSIONS THAT KEEP CIVILIZATION RUNNING

When people talk about "jobs the future can't replace," they usually imagine advanced technology or rare expertise. They overlook something far more durable: municipal work.

Cities, towns, and counties do not function on innovation alone. They function because someone shows up—every day—to enforce rules, keep records, remove waste, respond to emergencies, and maintain order. These roles are not glamorous. They are not portable. And they are almost impossible to automate away.

Firefighters, police officers, sanitation workers, and municipal clerks operate where law, physical reality, and human judgment collide. Their authority is local. Their work is embodied. Their mistakes have immediate consequences. That combination makes them uniquely resistant to abstraction, outsourcing, and AI replacement.

Automation can optimize dispatch routes. Software can flag anomalies in reports. AI can help analyze patterns. But when a building is burning, a street is blocked, a record must be certified, or a crisis unfolds in real time, someone still has to be there—vested with authority, accountable to the public, and trusted to act.

Municipal careers also share traits that are increasingly rare in the modern economy:

- Clear entry pathways
- Defined responsibilities
- Legal protections and due process
- Predictable advancement
- Pensions or long-term benefits tied to public service

These jobs do not scale globally. They cannot be offshored. They cannot be reduced to "content." They exist because communities exist.

This section explores municipal careers that are often dismissed as ordinary, outdated, or unambitious—but which in reality form the institutional spine of modern life. For people seeking stability, purpose, and work that still matters in a highly automated world, municipal service remains one of the most reliable paths forward.

Profile 15

FIREFIGHTER

What the Profession Does

Firefighters respond to fires, medical emergencies, hazardous material incidents, vehicle accidents, and natural disasters. The work extends far beyond extinguishing fires. Firefighters stabilize trauma patients, conduct rescues, enforce fire codes, educate the public, and operate complex equipment under extreme conditions.

Modern firefighters are trained generalists operating in unpredictable, high-risk environments. They make rapid decisions that affect lives, property, and public safety, often with incomplete information and no margin for error.

Why This Career Survives AI

Firefighting exists at the intersection of physical danger, moral responsibility, and real-time judgment—a space AI cannot occupy.

AI can assist with fire modeling, dispatch optimization, building sensors, and predictive risk analysis. It cannot enter a burning structure, assess human behavior under panic, improvise rescues, or assume legal responsibility for life-and-death decisions.

Firefighters are granted authority precisely because communities need trusted humans to act decisively when systems fail, conditions change, or chaos erupts. As long as people live in physical spaces and emergencies occur, firefighters remain indispensable.

Training, Certifications, and Entry Pathway

Entry requirements vary by jurisdiction but typically include:

- High school diploma or GED
- Valid driver's license
- Minimum age requirement (often 18–21)
- Physical agility and medical examinations
- Background check and psychological screening

Many departments give preference to candidates with EMT certification, military service, or prior public safety experience.

Training and Certification Path

Most firefighters complete a fire academy, either through:

- A municipal department, or
- A community college or regional fire training program

Core training includes:

- Fire suppression techniques
- Emergency medical response (often EMT-

Basic or higher)

- Rescue operations
- Hazardous materials awareness
- Equipment operation and safety

Continuing education is mandatory throughout a firefighter's career, with frequent recertification and skills testing.

Licensing

Firefighter certification is typically issued at the state level, with credentials such as:

- Firefighter I / Firefighter II
- EMT or Paramedic licensure

Licensing requirements vary by state but are standardized enough to allow lateral movement between departments with additional training.

Oversight, Regulation, and Accountability

Firefighters operate under:

- Municipal or county governments
- State fire marshals or certification boards
- Federal safety standards (OSHA, NFPA guidelines)

Accountability is formal and continuous. Performance is evaluated through drills, incident reviews, certifications, and internal discipline systems. Firefighters are personally accountable for adherence to safety protocols and operational command structures.

Compensation and Stability

Firefighting offers exceptional job stability, particularly in unionized or civil service systems.

Entry-level pay varies by region

Overtime and specialty certifications increase earnings.

Benefits often include healthcare, disability coverage, and pensions

While not universally high-paying, firefighting provides long-term financial predictability that is increasingly rare in private-sector employment.

Who This Careeer is For

Firefighters who thrive tend to be:

- Calm under pressure
- Physically capable and safety-conscious
- Team-oriented and disciplined
- Comfortable with structured authority
- Motivated by service rather than status

This career is well-suited for individuals who value purpose, camaraderie, and tangible impact over flexibility or remote work.

The Bigger Picture

Firefighting sits at the intersection of technology, judgment, and moral responsibility in a way few professions do. Modern fire departments use advanced tools—thermal imaging, predictive modeling, drones, building information systems—but when a structure is burning or a hillside is moving with wind and flame, decisions still come down to human beings operating under uncertainty.

No algorithm enters a smoke-filled room. No machine weighs the value of time against the value of life. No system assumes responsibility when conditions change faster than data can be processed.

Firefighters are trusted not because they follow instructions, but because they improvise under pressure while accepting personal risk on behalf of the public. That trust is not abstract; it is earned repeatedly, face to face, in moments when people are most vulnerable. This is the kind of trust that cannot be automated or outsourced.

As climate change drives longer wildfire seasons, denser urban development increases structural fire complexity, and aging infrastructure creates new hazards, the need for skilled firefighters is increasing—not decreasing. At the same time, the profession is quietly evolving. Firefighters today are also emergency medical responders, hazardous materials technicians, wildfire specialists, and infrastructure risk managers. The job has expanded, not narrowed.

Importantly, firefighting remains a profession where entry is not controlled by elite academic gatekeeping. Training is rigorous, physical, and ongoing, but it is grounded in certification, apprenticeship, and real-world performance rather than abstract credentials. Competence is visible. Failure is immediate. Reputation matters.

In an AI-driven economy that increasingly separates decision-makers from consequences, firefighters represent the opposite model: embodied work, local accountability, and direct service. They remind us that some careers endure not because they resist technology, but because technology cannot replace the human obligation at their core.

Firefighters are not relics of a pre-digital age. They are evidence that the future of work still depends on courage, skill, and judgment exercised in the real world.

Profile 16

POLICE OFFICER

What the Profession Does

Police officers enforce laws, maintain public order, respond to emergencies, investigate crimes, and protect individuals and property. Their work ranges from routine patrol and traffic enforcement to crisis intervention, domestic disputes, and violent crime response.

Modern policing requires constant judgment under uncertainty. Officers must assess intent, de-escalate conflict, apply force only when legally justified, document actions precisely, and operate within strict procedural and constitutional limits.

Why This Career Survives AI

Policing is fundamentally about human judgment, legal authority, and accountability.

AI can analyze data, identify patterns, assist with surveillance review, and improve resource allocation. It cannot interpret human behavior in real time, exercise lawful discretion, testify in court, or assume moral and legal responsibility for use-of-force decisions.

Police authority is granted by the state and constrained by law. That authority must be exercised by identifiable humans who can be trained, certified, supervised, disciplined, and held accountable. As long as societies require enforcement of laws in physical space, police officers remain irreplaceable.

Training, Certifications, and Entry Path

Requirements vary by jurisdiction but commonly include:

- High school diploma or GED (some departments prefer or require college credits)
- Minimum age (typically 20–21)
- Valid driver's license
- Clean or limited criminal history
- Physical fitness and medical clearance
- Psychological evaluation and background investigation
- Military service or prior public safety experience is often viewed favorably.

Training and Certification Path

Police officers must complete a state-approved police academy, either:

Sponsored by a department, or

Through a regional or college-based law enforcement program

Training typically covers:

- Criminal and constitutional law
- Defensive tactics and use of force
- Firearms proficiency
- Emergency vehicle operations
- Report writing and evidence handling

- De-escalation and crisis intervention

Ongoing in-service training and periodic recertification are mandatory.

Licensing

Police officers are licensed or certified at the state level, often through a Peace Officer Standards and Training (POST) authority or equivalent.

Licensing is conditional and can be suspended or revoked for misconduct, failure to maintain training standards, or criminal violations. Lateral transfers between departments usually require additional certification or probationary periods.

Oversight, Regulation, and Accountability

Policing is among the most heavily regulated professions in the public sector. Oversight includes:

- Departmental command structures
- State certification boards
- Internal affairs investigations
- Civilian review processes (in many jurisdictions)
- Judicial review and court testimony

Every action may be reviewed, recorded, audited, and challenged. Accountability is formal, ongoing, and increasingly transparent.

Compensation and Stability

Police work offers high employment stability, particularly within civil service systems.

Salaries vary widely by region and agency

Overtime, specialty units, and seniority increase earnings

Benefits typically include healthcare, disability coverage, and pensions

While the profession carries unique stresses, it remains one of the more economically secure non-degree career paths available.

Who This Career is For.

Officers who thrive tend to be:

- Emotionally controlled and resilient
- Comfortable with conflict and authority
- Strong communicators under stress
- Detail-oriented and procedurally disciplined
- Motivated by service and public order

This career suits individuals who can balance empathy with enforcement, and discretion with accountability.

The Bigger Picture

Policing is fundamentally a judgment profession. Laws may be written in code and procedures captured in policy manuals, but enforcement happens in real time, among people, under conditions that are rarely clear and often volatile.

Technology can assist—body cameras, databases, predictive tools—but it cannot replace discretion. Every call requires human assessment: intent, risk, credibility, proportionality. These are not computational problems. They are moral ones, carried out in public, with consequences that cannot be undone.

As social tensions rise and institutions strain, the demand for capable, well-trained officers does not disappear—it becomes more acute. The role is evolving toward de-escalation, crisis response, and community-based decision-making, not away from it. That evolution increases the need for judgment, not less.

Policing remains one of the few careers where authority is delegated directly by society, not mediated by credentials or distance. Trust is fragile, earned locally, and lost quickly. No system can automate legitimacy.

In an economy increasingly shaped by remote work and abstract outcomes, police officers represent a profession grounded in presence, accountability, and immediate responsibility—work that endures because it must.

Profile 17

EMERGENCY MANAGEMENT OFFICIAL

What the Profession Does

Emergency Management Officials plan for, coordinate, and oversee responses to natural disasters, public health emergencies, infrastructure failures, and large-scale incidents. Their work spans preparedness, response, recovery, and mitigation—often referred to as the full emergency management cycle.

They develop emergency operations plans, coordinate between police, fire, medical services, utilities, and elected officials, manage emergency operations centers, and act as the central organizing authority when routine systems are overwhelmed.

Much of the work happens before a crisis occurs. When disasters strike, Emergency Management Officials become the connective tissue that keeps institutions functioning.

Why This Career Survives AI

Emergency management depends on coordination, authority, and judgment under uncertainty.

AI can model risks, analyze weather data, simulate scenarios, and assist with logistics. It cannot negotiate jurisdictional conflicts, prioritize competing human needs, brief elected leaders, or adapt plans in real time when assumptions fail.

Emergencies are not technical puzzles alone—they are social, political, and ethical events. Communities require identifiable human leaders who can assume responsibility, communicate clearly, and make consequential decisions amid chaos. That necessity makes emergency management resistant to automation.

Training, Certifications, and Entry Path.

Entry requirements vary widely by jurisdiction but commonly include:

- High school diploma or GED (many positions prefer college coursework or degrees)
- Experience in public safety, military, utilities, public administration, or related fields
- Strong communication and organizational skills

Many Emergency Management Officials transition from fire service, law enforcement, military service, or public works rather than entering directly from school.

Training and Certification Path

Training typically includes a mix of formal coursework and practical experience:

- FEMA Incident Command System (ICS) training
- National Incident Management System (NIMS) certification
- Emergency Operations Center (EOC) management training

- Hazard mitigation and disaster recovery planning
- Advanced roles may require:
- State emergency management certification
- FEMA Professional Development Series (PDS)
- Continuing education tied to evolving federal and state standards

Training is ongoing and often mandatory.

Licensing

Unlike some public safety roles, emergency management is not always licensed in the traditional sense. Instead, qualification is established through:

- State-recognized certifications
- FEMA and DHS credentialing
- Employer-specific authorization

Authority is conferred through appointment rather than license, but credentials must be maintained to remain eligible for federal and state coordination roles.

Oversight, Regulation, and Accountability

Emergency Management Officials operate under:

- Municipal, county, or state governments
- Federal coordination frameworks (FEMA, DHS)
- Statutory emergency powers defined by law

Their actions are subject to after-action reviews, audits, public records laws, and legislative oversight. Performance during crises is scrutinized closely, often with political and legal consequences.

Compensation and Stability

Emergency management offers strong job stability, particularly in regions prone to disasters.

Salaries vary by jurisdiction and responsibility level

Positions are often salaried with government benefits

Demand is steady and increasing due to climate, infrastructure aging, and population growth

While not immune to budget pressures, emergency management roles are rarely eliminated and often expanded after major incidents.

Who this Career is For.

This career is for people who think in systems rather than moments. Emergency management officials are not first responders in the traditional sense; they are planners, coordinators, and decision-makers who operate before, during, and long after a crisis unfolds. The work rewards those who can anticipate problems, organize resources, and remain steady when events overwhelm normal procedures.

It suits individuals who are comfortable working behind the scenes, where success often looks like problems that never happen. Much of the job involves planning, documentation, training exercises, and interagency coordination—often invisible until something goes wrong. Recognition is rare; responsibility is constant.

Strong candidates tend to be calm under pressure, skilled communicators, and pragmatic problem-solvers. They must translate between technical experts, political leaders, first responders, and the public—often in high-stress environments where information is incomplete and time is limited. Patience, credibility, and emotional control matter as much as technical knowledge.

This career is well-suited for people with backgrounds in public safety, the military, logistics, infrastructure, healthcare, or local government, but it is also accessible to those willing to build expertise through certification and experience rather than formal degrees alone. What matters most is reliability, judgment, and the ability to coordinate action across complex systems.

Emergency management is for those who want meaningful responsibility without spectacle—people motivated by public service, long-term resilience, and the quiet satisfaction of helping communities endure their worst days and recover afterward.

The Bigger Picture

Emergency management is the connective tissue of public safety. When disasters occur—natural or man-made—no single agency is in charge. Police, fire, hospitals, utilities, transportation, and elected officials all operate simultaneously. Emergency managers exist to make that complexity function.

This is not a profession of reaction alone. The most

important work happens long before an emergency begins: risk assessment, continuity planning, training exercises, and interagency agreements. When these systems fail, the consequences are visible. When they succeed, the public rarely notices.

As climate change intensifies storms, wildfires, heat events, and flooding—and as infrastructure ages and populations grow more interconnected—the role of emergency management becomes more central, not less. Technology can model scenarios and move information, but it cannot create coordination, trust, or authority across institutions. Those remain human responsibilities.

Emergency management officials operate in a space where decisions carry political, economic, and human consequences. They must balance speed with legitimacy, planning with adaptability, and public communication with operational reality. These tradeoffs cannot be automated.

In an economy increasingly focused on individual productivity, emergency management represents a different kind of value: collective resilience. It is a profession that endures because complex societies require people whose sole job is to prepare for disruption—and to hold systems together when disruption arrives.

Profile 18

CODE ENFORCEMENT OFFICER

What The Profession Does.

Code Enforcement Officers ensure that buildings, properties, and land uses comply with local, state, and sometimes federal codes. Their work covers housing standards, zoning regulations, nuisance violations, safety hazards, and quality-of-life issues that affect entire communities.

They investigate complaints, conduct inspections, document violations, issue notices and citations, coordinate with other departments, and work with property owners to achieve compliance. The role blends technical knowledge, fieldwork, documentation, and public interaction.

Why This Career Survives AI

Code enforcement operates at the intersection of law, physical space, and human discretion.

AI can flag potential violations using data, satellite imagery, or reports. It cannot walk a property, assess conditions in context, interpret intent, negotiate compliance, or testify credibly in administrative hearings or court.

Code Enforcement Officers carry delegated legal authority and must apply rules consistently while exercising judgment. Because enforcement decisions affect property rights, health, and safety, they must be made by accountable humans, not automated systems.

Training, Certifications and Entry Path.

Entry Requirements

Requirements vary by jurisdiction but typically include:

- High school diploma or GED
- Valid driver's license
- Background check
- Strong written and verbal communication skills

Some agencies prefer experience in construction, inspection, law enforcement, or public administration. A college degree is sometimes listed but rarely mandatory.

Training and Certification Path

Most Code Enforcement Officers receive:

- On-the-job training specific to local ordinances
- State or regional code enforcement certification courses
- Common training areas include:
- Building and housing codes
- Zoning and land-use regulations
- Inspection techniques
- Report writing and evidence documentation
- Conflict management and legal procedures

Continuing education is usually required as codes evolve.

Licensing

Licensing and certification are often handled at the state or regional level, with credentials such as:

- Certified Code Enforcement Officer
- Property Maintenance Inspector
- Zoning Enforcement Certification

Licenses may be required for certain inspection activities and must be maintained through continuing education.

Oversight, Regulation, and Accountability

Code Enforcement Officers operate under:

- Municipal or county governments
- Local ordinances enacted by elected officials
- Administrative law and due process requirements

Their actions are subject to appeal, review by supervisors, and scrutiny in administrative hearings or court. Documentation, consistency, and procedural fairness are essential to the role.

Compensation and Stability

Code enforcement offers steady employment and predictable schedules.

Salaries vary by region and complexity of duties

Positions are typically full-time with government benefits

Demand is stable, tied directly to population and development

Because communities are legally obligated to

enforce their own codes, these positions are rarely eliminated.

Who This Career is For.

Those who thrive tend to be:

- Detail-oriented and observant
- Comfortable enforcing rules calmly and fairly
- Strong communicators, especially in difficult conversations
- Independent yet procedurally disciplined
- Motivated by public safety and community standards

This role suits individuals who prefer measured authority, fieldwork, and tangible local impact over crisis response or desk-only work.

The Bigger Picture.

Code enforcement is where laws meet the physical world. Building, zoning, health, and safety codes exist to prevent harm before it occurs, but they only matter if someone interprets, applies, and enforces them on the ground. Code enforcement officers are the quiet regulators of everyday life, working upstream of emergencies and disasters.

This is a profession built on judgment rather than force. No two properties, violations, or communities are the same. Officers must balance compliance with fairness, public safety with economic reality, and written regulations with human circumstances. Technology can flag violations and track cases, but it cannot determine intent, credibility, or proportional response.

As cities densify, housing ages, and climate pressures increase stress on buildings and infrastructure, the role of code enforcement becomes more critical. Fire risk, structural failure, illegal conversions, and environmental hazards are all managed—or missed—at this level. When enforcement fails, the consequences surface later as fires, collapses, health crises, or displacement.

Code enforcement also operates at the boundary between government authority and private property, a space where legitimacy matters. Compliance depends less on punishment than on trust, consistency, and the officer's ability to explain why rules exist and how to meet them. That legitimacy cannot be automated.

In an AI-driven economy focused on speed and scale, code enforcement represents a slower but essential function: safeguarding communities through local knowledge, discretion, and accountability. It is work that persists because prevention, unlike automation, depends on human judgment exercised in real places.

Profile 19

SANITARIAN
(Public Health Inspector / Environmental Health Specialist)

What the Profession Does

Sanitarians protect public health by inspecting and regulating food service establishments, water systems, wastewater disposal, solid waste operations, and other environmental health factors. Their work helps prevent disease outbreaks, contamination, and long-term environmental harm.

They conduct inspections, collect samples, enforce health codes, investigate complaints, respond to suspected public health threats, and educate businesses and the public on compliance. Much of their work happens quietly—successful sanitation is invisible because crises are prevented before they occur.

Why This Career Survives AI

Sanitation is rooted in field inspection, judgment, and legal enforcement.

AI can assist with data analysis, trend detection, and scheduling. It cannot smell spoiled food, observe unsafe practices, assess sanitation in context, or exercise enforcement authority with discretion.

Sanitarians operate under statutory authority and must make defensible decisions that affect businesses, public safety, and legal outcomes. Because their work involves physical environments and regulatory judgment, it cannot be fully automated.

Traings, Certifications, and Entry Path

Entry Requirements

Requirements vary by state and county but commonly include:

- High school diploma or GED
- Coursework or experience in environmental health, biology, chemistry, or related fields (often preferred)
- Valid driver's license
- Background check

Some jurisdictions require a bachelor's degree, while others allow entry through experience and certification.

Training and Certification Path

Training typically includes:

- On-the-job training with experienced inspectors
- State-approved environmental health training programs
- Food safety certification (such as ServSafe or equivalent)

Continuing education is required to stay current with evolving health regulations and scientific standards.

Licensing

Sanitarians are often licensed or registered at the state level, under titles such as:

- Registered Sanitarian (RS)
- Registered Environmental Health Specialist (REHS)

Licensing requires passing an exam and maintaining continuing education credits.

Oversight, Regulation, and Accountability

Sanitarians operate under:

- Local and state public health departments
- State health agencies
- Federal guidelines (CDC, EPA, FDA Food Code)

Their work is subject to audits, appeals, legal challenges, and public records laws. Inspection reports must be accurate, defensible, and consistent.

Compensation and Stability

Sanitarian positions offer stable, predictable employment.

Salaries vary by region and education requirements

Positions are typically full-time with government benefits

Demand remains steady due to population growth, regulatory requirements, and public health risks

Public health infrastructure is rarely dismantled, even during economic downturns.

Who This Career is For

Those who thrive tend to be:

- Observant and detail-oriented
- Comfortable enforcing regulations calmly
- Interested in science and public health
- Strong communicators and educators
- Independent workers with high integrity

This role suits individuals who prefer preventive impact, structured authority, and steady fieldwork over crisis response or desk-only roles.

The Bigger Picture

Sanitarians operate at the boundary between public health and everyday life. Long before illness becomes visible, their work quietly reduces risk—through inspections, enforcement, education, and prevention. When sanitation systems fail, the consequences are immediate and widespread. When they succeed, nothing happens, and that is the point.

This profession is fundamentally preventive. Sanitarians protect communities from foodborne illness, water contamination, waste mismanagement, and environmental health hazards that rarely make headlines but shape quality of life. Their authority is technical, local, and continuous, exercised not in emergencies but in the routines that keep populations healthy.

Technology can assist with data collection, testing,

and recordkeeping, but it cannot replace on-site judgment. Determining whether a kitchen is safe, a water source is compromised, or a housing condition poses a health risk requires human observation, discretion, and the ability to interpret regulations in context. These decisions often involve negotiation, education, and trust—not automation.

As populations grow denser, infrastructure ages, and climate pressures strain water, food, and waste systems, the role of sanitarians becomes more critical. Public health threats increasingly emerge from ordinary systems pushed beyond their limits. Preventing these failures requires professionals who understand both regulation and reality.

In an economy focused on innovation and visibility, sanitarians represent a quieter form of resilience. Their work endures because public health, at its core, depends not on technology alone, but on people whose responsibility is to prevent harm before it occurs—and to do so consistently, locally, and without recognition.

Profile 20

PARKS MANAGER

What The Profession Does.

A parks manager oversees the operation, maintenance, and long-term stewardship of public parks, open spaces, and recreational facilities. Depending on jurisdiction, this may include city parks, county open space, regional trail systems, or state-managed lands. The role combines land management, infrastructure oversight, budgeting, personnel supervision, and public engagement.

Day-to-day responsibilities often include supervising maintenance crews, managing contracts, coordinating with environmental and public safety agencies, addressing public complaints, and ensuring compliance with environmental, safety, and accessibility regulations. Parks managers also plan capital improvements such as trail construction, irrigation systems, playgrounds, and habitat restoration projects.

Beyond operations, parks managers serve as custodians of public land. They make decisions about use, preservation, and risk—decisions that shape how communities interact with shared spaces over decades.

Why This Career Survives AI

Parks management depends on judgment exercised in physical, ecological, and political contexts that cannot be abstracted into software. While AI can assist with mapping, scheduling, and environmental monitoring, it cannot decide how land should be balanced between conservation, access, safety, and public demand.

Much of the work involves navigating competing interests: recreation versus habitat protection, budget limits versus maintenance needs, public expectations versus ecological limits. These are not optimization problems with clear answers. They require negotiation, discretion, and accountability.

Parks managers are also embedded locally. They rely on firsthand knowledge of land conditions, seasonal patterns, community behavior, and long-term environmental change. AI can provide data, but it cannot replace responsibility for outcomes that unfold slowly and visibly in the real world.

Training, Certifications, and Entry Path

Entry paths vary by jurisdiction, but parks managers typically rise through experience rather than formal academic gatekeeping. Many begin in maintenance, groundskeeping, forestry, recreation coordination, or environmental services roles before advancing into supervisory and managerial positions.

Common qualifications include certifications in park

and recreation management, public administration, environmental management, or arboriculture. Some positions require or prefer coursework or degrees, but many emphasize demonstrated competence, supervisory experience, and familiarity with public-sector operations.

Ongoing training is common and often required, including safety certifications, environmental compliance, wildfire mitigation, and emergency coordination. Advancement is usually tied to experience, performance, and civil service examinations rather than credentials alone.

Compensation and Stability

Compensation varies by region and level of responsibility but generally offers stable, middle-income earnings with strong benefits. Salaries often increase predictably with tenure, promotion, and union-negotiated contracts.

While parks management is not a high-paying career, it offers exceptional stability. Positions are typically funded through municipal, county, or state budgets and are less vulnerable to market volatility or automation-driven disruption.

Benefits often include pensions, healthcare, paid leave, and long-term job security—features increasingly rare in the private sector.

Who This Career Is For

This career is well-suited for people who value stewardship over visibility and long-term outcomes over short-term metrics. Successful parks managers are practical, patient, and comfortable working within bureaucratic systems while still solving real-world problems.

It appeals to those who enjoy working with land, infrastructure, and people simultaneously. Strong candidates are steady decision-makers, effective communicators, and capable supervisors who can balance environmental concerns with public access and political realities.

Parks management is ideal for individuals motivated by public service and continuity—people who want their work to matter quietly, over time, rather than dramatically or immediately.

The Bigger Picture

Parks management is governance expressed through land. Public parks are not amenities alone; they are infrastructure—supporting public health, environmental resilience, and social cohesion.

As climate change intensifies drought, wildfire risk, flooding, and ecological stress, parks managers increasingly function as risk managers and environmental stewards. Their decisions affect fire behavior, water retention, habitat survival, and community safety.

In an economy focused on speed, growth, and digital abstraction, parks managers represent a different model of value: preservation over time. This profession endures because livable societies depend on people whose job is not extraction or optimization, but guardianship of shared spaces.

Parks management is governance expressed through land. While often perceived as maintenance or recreation, the role of a parks manager sits at the intersection of ecology, public access, infrastructure, and long-term stewardship. These are not abstract responsibilities; they play out in soil, water, trees, trails, and people.

Technology can assist with mapping, scheduling, and environmental monitoring, but it cannot decide how land should be used, protected, or shared. Parks managers constantly balance competing interests: conservation versus access, safety versus openness, budget constraints versus public expectation. These decisions are contextual, political, and deeply human.

As climate change intensifies droughts, wildfires, floods, and invasive species pressures, public lands are becoming frontline infrastructure. Parks managers increasingly function as risk managers—overseeing fire mitigation, erosion control, habitat preservation, and emergency coordination—often with limited resources and high public scrutiny.

This profession also operates on trust. Parks are shared civic spaces, and their legitimacy depends on consistent, visible stewardship. When management succeeds, the public experiences continuity and care. When it fails, degradation is immediate and often irreversible. No automated system can replace local knowledge of land, users, and ecological limits.

In an economy focused on speed, extraction, and digital abstraction, parks management represents a slower but essential form of value creation:

preservation over time. It endures because societies that wish to remain livable must invest in people whose job is not growth, but guardianship.

MUNICIPAL CAREERS AND THE LIMITS OF AUTOMATION

Municipal careers share a defining characteristic that separates them from much of the modern labor market: they exist because communities cannot outsource themselves.

Firefighters, police officers, emergency managers, code enforcement officers, sanitarians, clerks, and county officials do not compete in global markets. They operate within clearly defined jurisdictions, under law, and with authority granted by the public. Their work is bound to physical places, legal processes, and human judgment.

This combination makes municipal careers unusually resistant to automation.

AI can assist with analysis, recordkeeping, scheduling, and prediction. It can improve efficiency and reduce clerical burden. What it cannot do is assume legal responsibility, exercise discretion under uncertainty, or be held accountable by citizens, courts, or voters. Municipal work requires all three.

Across these professions, a common pattern emerges:

- Authority is delegated by law, not by employer preference
- Errors carry public consequences, not just private costs
- Accountability is continuous and visible
- Work persists regardless of economic cycles

Municipal roles are not immune to change, but they are insulated from disappearance. Cities still burn, laws still require enforcement, food must remain safe, records must be accurate, and disasters must be managed—even when technology fails or budgets tighten.

These careers also challenge a modern misconception: that resilience comes from flexibility alone. In municipal work, resilience comes from embeddedness. The job exists because the community exists.

For individuals seeking stable, non-abstract work with clear boundaries and real impact, municipal careers offer something increasingly rare: durable relevance. They do not scale upward or outward, but they endure.

In a future shaped by AI and automation, the most secure roles may not be the most advanced, but the most indispensable. Municipal careers survive not by outpacing technology, but by occupying spaces technology cannot lawfully, ethically, or physically enter.

That is not a flaw in these professions. It is their strength.

Chapter 4

Industrial and Field Systems: Where Reality Pushes Back

Modern economies are often described as digital, automated, and knowledge-based. This description is incomplete.

Behind every finished product, every shipment, every functioning supply chain, there exists a world of machines, materials, and physical processes that must be kept within narrow tolerances to avoid failure. These systems do not behave politely. They vibrate, overheat, corrode, clog, fatigue, and break. When they do, someone must diagnose the problem and intervene—on site, in real time.

The professions in this section operate where theory gives way to reality. They work with engines, pipelines, heavy equipment, control systems, and industrial environments that cannot be paused, rebooted, or safely experimented on. Their success is measured not by innovation, but by continuity.

Automation plays an important role here, but it does not eliminate the need for skilled human operators and technicians. Industrial systems are layered over decades of legacy equipment, incremental upgrades, and site-specific modifications. Documentation is imperfect. Conditions vary. When something behaves in an unexpected way, judgment matters more than optimization.

These careers also reveal another misconception about technological progress: that complexity reduces human involvement. In practice, complexity often increases it. The more tightly coupled a system becomes, the more dangerous small errors are—and the more valuable experienced humans become when something deviates from the expected.

Like healthcare and infrastructure, industrial and field systems are governed by safety rules, regulatory oversight, and liability. Someone must be accountable when a pressure vessel fails, a machine malfunctions, or a process goes out of control. Algorithms may advise. Sensors may alert. But responsibility remains human.

Most of the professions that follow do not require elite credentials. They require technical skill, situational awareness, and the willingness to work where conditions are loud, dirty, or uncomfortable. They reward competence, patience, and problem-solving under constraint.

As artificial intelligence advances, work that remains anchored to the physical world—subject to friction, force, and failure—will persist. Not because it resists technology, but because it exists where technology alone is insufficient.

The chapters that follow examine careers that keep industry running when ideal conditions disappear. They are not abstract. They are not remote. And when they fail, the consequences are immediate.

Profile 21

Heavy Equipment Field Technician

What The Profession Does.

Heavy Equipment Field Technicians diagnose, repair, and maintain the machines that move earth, build infrastructure, extract resources, and keep industrial operations running. They service excavators, loaders, bulldozers, cranes, graders, haul trucks, and other large equipment used in construction, mining, forestry, agriculture, and energy.

Unlike shop-based mechanics, field technicians travel directly to job sites—often remote, muddy, noisy, or weather-exposed—to repair equipment where it fails. They troubleshoot hydraulic systems, diesel engines, electrical controls, drivetrains, and computerized diagnostics, frequently under time pressure and production demands.

When heavy equipment stops, work stops. Entire projects can hinge on a single repair.

Why This Career Survives AI

Heavy equipment maintenance exists where weight, force, dirt, and improvisation dominate.

AI can assist with diagnostics and predictive maintenance, but it cannot:

- Physically access broken machines in

uncontrolled environments
- Perform complex mechanical and hydraulic repairs on site
- Adapt to undocumented modifications and wear
- Balance safety, speed, and operational constraints in the field
- Accept responsibility for equipment returned to service

Field failures rarely resemble training scenarios. Machines break unevenly, under load, and often far from ideal conditions. Technicians must decide what can be repaired immediately, what can be safely deferred, and what requires shutdown.

This work rewards experience and judgment, not abstraction.

Training, Certification, and Entry Path

Heavy Equipment Field Technicians typically enter through trade-based pathways.

Common entry routes include:
- Apprenticeships or employer sponsored training
- Technical or vocational programs in diesel or heavy equipment technology
- Military or industrial maintenance backgrounds

Certifications may include:
- Manufacturer-specific training

- Diesel and hydraulic systems credentials
- Safety and equipment operation certifications

Four-year degrees are rarely required. Advancement depends on competence, versatility, and reliability.

Compensation and Stability

Heavy Equipment Field Technicians earn strong incomes, particularly with experience.

- Typical pay range: $65,000–$100,000+ annually
- Overtime and travel premiums common
- High demand in construction, mining, energy, and infrastructure sectors
- Skills transferable across industries and regions

Physical economies still require physical machines.

Who This Career Is For

This profession is well suited to individuals who:

- Are mechanically inclined and comfortable with problem-solving
- Can work independently in difficult environments
- Prefer hands-on work over office settings
- Are trusted to make safety-critical decisions
- Value skill over status

It attracts people who are comfortable being the one called when nothing else works.

The Bigger Picture

Heavy Equipment Field Technicians keep the physical economy moving. Roads, bridges, mines, power plants, pipelines, and forests all depend on machines that eventually fail—and on humans who can bring them back to life.

In conversations about automation and smart machinery, this profession offers a grounding reminder:

When something weighs forty tons, reality sets the rules.

Profile 22

Industrial Instrumentation Technician (Instrumentation & Controls Technician / I&C Technician)

What The Profession Does.

Industrial Instrumentation Technicians install, calibrate, troubleshoot, and maintain the sensors and control systems that regulate industrial processes. They work with pressure, temperature, flow, level, and analytical instruments that govern how factories, power plants, refineries, water systems, and manufacturing lines operate.

Their responsibilities include testing and calibrating instruments, diagnosing signal faults, maintaining control loops, verifying safety interlocks, and ensuring that automated systems respond correctly to real-world conditions. They work closely with operators, engineers, and maintenance crews to keep complex processes stable and safe.

If automation is the nervous system of industry, instrumentation technicians are the ones who ensure it is telling the truth.

Why This Career Survives AI

Instrumentation is where automation depends on humans rather than replacing them.

AI cannot:

- Verify that sensors are physically installed correctly
- Calibrate instruments against real-world reference standards
- Diagnose faults caused by vibration, corrosion, moisture, or wiring errors
- Resolve discrepancies between what the system reports and what is actually happening
- Accept responsibility for safety-critical control failures

Industrial automation assumes accurate inputs. When sensors drift, fail, or lie, automated systems can make catastrophic decisions. Determining whether a reading is real, distorted, or dangerous requires human judgment at the point of measurement.

Ironically, the more automated a system becomes, the more valuable skilled instrumentation technicians are.

Training, Certification, and Entry Path

Instrumentation Technicians typically enter through technical training rather than academic pathways.

Common routes include:

- Technical or vocational programs in instrumentation and controls
- Apprenticeships or employer-based training
- Electrical, industrial maintenance, or military technical backgrounds

Certifications may include:

- ISA (International Society of Automation) credentials
- Manufacturer-specific control system training
- Electrical and safety certifications
- Four-year degrees are usually not required

Advancement depends on precision, troubleshooting skill, and reliability.

Compensation and Stability

Industrial Instrumentation Technicians earn strong, stable incomes with excellent demand.

- Typical pay range: $70,000–$110,000+ annually
- Higher pay in energy, chemicals, power generation, and advanced manufacturing
- Day, shift, and on-call work depending on facility
- Long-term relevance as automation expands

Automation does not eliminate this role—it locks it in.

Who This Career Is For

This profession is well suited to individuals who:

- Enjoy precision and systematic problem-solving
- Are comfortable with electronics and industrial systems

- Can think abstractly while working physically
- Prefer quiet authority over visible control
- Take responsibility seriously

It attracts people who understand that bad data is worse than no data.

The Bigger Picture

Industrial Instrumentation Technicians occupy a paradoxical position in modern industry. They are surrounded by automation, yet automation fails without them. Their work determines whether machines respond intelligently—or dangerously.

In discussions about AI-driven industry, this profession exposes a reality that often goes unspoken:

Automation only works when humans verify reality.

Profile 23

Pipeline Operator

What The Profession Does.

Pipeline Operators monitor and control the systems that transport oil, natural gas, refined fuels, water, and other critical materials over long distances. From control rooms and field stations, they regulate pressure, flow rates, pump and compressor stations, and valves to ensure continuous, safe operation.

They respond to alarms, coordinate maintenance, isolate sections during failures, and execute emergency shutdowns when leaks or pressure anomalies occur. Many operators also conduct field inspections, verify instrumentation, and work with emergency responders and regulators during incidents.

When pipelines work, nothing happens. When they fail, the consequences are immediate, environmental, and political.

Why This Career Survives AI

Pipeline operations are high-risk, tightly regulated, and legally exposed—conditions that require human judgment.

AI can assist with leak detection, predictive analytics, and optimization, but it cannot:

- Make irreversible shutdown decisions under

uncertainty
- Balance safety, supply continuity, and downstream impacts
- Interpret ambiguous sensor data during evolving events
- Coordinate human crews, regulators, and emergency services
- Accept legal and criminal liability for failures

Pipelines run through varied terrain, aging infrastructure, and communities. Sensor data is never perfect. When alarms trigger, operators must decide whether to stop flow, isolate sections, or escalate—often with incomplete information.

When mistakes can cause explosions, contamination, or loss of life, humans remain in control by necessity.

Training, Certification, and Entry Path

Pipeline Operators typically enter through employer-based training programs.

Common requirements include:
- High school diploma or GED
- On-the-job training and qualification progression
- Safety and regulatory compliance training

Some operators come from:
- Military operations
- Industrial or power plant operations
- Maintenance or instrumentation backgrounds

Formal four-year degrees are usually not required.

Advancement depends on procedural discipline, situational awareness, and trust.

Compensation and Stability

Pipeline Operators earn strong incomes with exceptional long-term stability.

- Typical pay range: $70,000–$120,000+ annually
- Shift work and on-call responsibilities common
- Strong benefits and overtime opportunities
- Demand persists regardless of economic cycles
- Energy and material transport do not pause.

Who This Career Is For

This profession is well suited to individuals who:

- Are calm under pressure
- Comfortable making high-impact decisions
- Detail-oriented and procedure-driven
- Willing to work shifts and nights
- Value responsibility over visibility

It attracts people trusted to act correctly when no one is watching.

The Bigger Picture

Pipeline Operators oversee some of the most consequential hidden systems in modern society. Their work determines whether energy and materials move safely—or catastrophically.

In conversations about smart infrastructure and automation, this profession reinforces a core truth:

When consequences are irreversible, someone must remain accountable.

Profile 24

Millwright

What The Profession Does.

Millwrights install, assemble, align, maintain, and repair industrial machinery used in manufacturing, energy production, mining, food processing, and heavy industry. They work with pumps, conveyors, turbines, compressors, presses, gearboxes, and custom-built mechanical systems—often machinery that must operate within extremely tight tolerances.

Their work includes precision alignment, vibration analysis, rigging and lifting, bearing replacement, shaft installation, and diagnosing mechanical failures. Millwrights frequently work during shutdowns, outages, or emergencies, when time pressure is high and mistakes are costly.

When machines vibrate, overheat, seize, or fail prematurely, millwrights are called to find out why—and fix it.

Why This Career Survives AI

Millwright work exists where precision meets unpredictability.

AI can assist with design, modeling, and predictive maintenance, but it cannot:

- Physically align heavy rotating equipment
- Feel vibration, resistance, or binding during installation
- Adapt to warped foundations, worn components, or undocumented modifications
- Safely rig and move massive machinery
- Take responsibility for equipment returned to service

Industrial machines rarely fail in textbook ways. Foundations shift. Components wear unevenly. Previous repairs introduce new variables. Millwrights must interpret physical reality—not just measurements—and make judgment calls that determine whether equipment runs smoothly or self-destructs.

This is tacit knowledge, earned through experience, not data alone.

Training, Certification, and Entry Path

Millwrights typically enter through formal apprenticeships or trade training programs.

Common pathways include:

- Apprenticeships (often 3–4 years)
- Union or employer-sponsored training
- Industrial maintenance or military backgrounds

Training covers:

- Mechanical systems and materials
- Precision measurement and alignment
- Rigging and lifting

- Safety and lockout/tagout procedures

Four-year college degrees are not required. Advancement depends on skill, accuracy, and safety record.

Compensation and Stability

Millwrights earn strong incomes with consistent demand across industries.

- Typical pay range: $65,000–$110,000+ annually
- Overtime common during shutdowns and outages
- Strong union presence in many regions
- Skills transferable across sectors and locations

As long as industry uses machines, millwrights remain essential.

Who This Career Is For

This profession is well suited to individuals who:

- Are mechanically precise and patient
- Enjoy solving complex physical problems
- Can work under pressure during critical outages
- Take pride in invisible accuracy
- Prefer mastery over management

It attracts people who understand that small misalignments cause large failures.

The Bigger Picture.

Millwrights are the translators between engineering intent and mechanical reality. They ensure that machines behave as designed—or compensate when reality intervenes.

In an age fascinated by digital twins and simulation, this profession reminds us:

Steel still obeys physics, not software.

Profile 25

Boiler Operator
(Stationary Engineer / Power Engineer — title varies by jurisdiction)

What The Profession Does.

Boiler Operators are responsible for operating, monitoring, and maintaining high-pressure boilers and related systems that produce steam, heat, or power for buildings and industrial facilities. They work in hospitals, universities, factories, refineries, power plants, ships, and large commercial buildings.

Their duties include controlling boiler pressure and temperature, managing fuel and water systems, monitoring gauges and alarms, performing routine inspections, maintaining auxiliary equipment (pumps, valves, compressors), and responding immediately to abnormal conditions.

Boilers concentrate enormous amounts of energy in confined spaces. When they are managed correctly, nothing happens. When they are not, the results can be catastrophic.

Why This Career Survives AI

Boiler operation is inherently hazardous, governed by physics that allow no margin for abstraction.

AI can assist with monitoring and optimization, but it cannot:

- Assume legal responsibility for pressure-vessel safety
- Respond correctly to rapidly evolving failure conditions
- Balance competing risks when procedures conflict with reality
- Perform physical inspections and emergency interventions
- Decide when to shut down systems that entire facilities depend on

Pressure systems do not fail politely. Sensors can lag or lie. Alarms can cascade. Operators must interpret what matters, what is noise, and what requires immediate action—often under time pressure.

That responsibility cannot be automated away.

Training, Certification, and Entry Path

Boiler Operators enter through licensing and experience, not academic prestige.

Typical requirements include:

- High school diploma or GED
- On-the-job training or apprenticeship
- State or municipal boiler/operator licenses

Licensing is often tiered (e.g., Third-Class to First-Class), with higher levels allowing operation of larger or more complex systems. Advancement is based on time in service, examinations, and demonstrated competence.

Four-year degrees are usually optional. Licensure, judgment, and reliability matter most.

Compensation and Stability

Boiler Operators earn solid incomes with exceptional long-term stability.

- Typical pay range: $60,000–$100,000+ annually
- Higher pay for high-pressure or large facilities
- Shift work and overtime common

Strong demand in healthcare, education, manufacturing, and energy
Boilers cannot be outsourced, digitized, or left unattended.

Who This Career Is For

This profession is well suited to individuals who:

- Are disciplined and attentive
- Comfortable with responsibility and routine
- Prefer controlled environments over chaos
- Follow procedures without losing situational awareness
- Take pride in quiet, error-free operation

It rewards people who understand that boring is good when explosions are possible.

The Bigger Picture

Boiler Operators manage some of the oldest—and most dangerous—technology still in continuous use. Steam powered the industrial revolution, and mishandled steam still kills.

In discussions about smart systems and autonomous control, this profession delivers a timeless reminder:

Pressure does not care how advanced your software is.

Profile 26

Industrial Electrician

What The Profession Does.

Industrial Electricians install, maintain, troubleshoot, and repair the electrical systems that power factories, processing plants, refineries, mines, power stations, and large industrial facilities. Their work spans motors, drives, control panels, switchgear, programmable logic controllers (PLCs), sensors, and safety systems.

Unlike residential or commercial electricians, industrial electricians work on live systems that cannot simply be shut down without stopping production or creating new hazards. They diagnose faults, trace wiring, interpret schematics, replace components, and restore systems under time pressure—often in noisy, hot, or hazardous environments.

When industrial electricity fails, machines stop, processes destabilize, and safety risks multiply.

Why This Career Survives AI

Industrial electrical work exists where automation itself requires constant human correction.

AI can assist with monitoring, diagnostics, and optimization, but it cannot:

- Safely work inside energized industrial systems
- Trace faults through layered, modified, and undocumented wiring
- Adapt repairs to real-world damage and degradation
- Balance production demands against electrical safety
- Accept responsibility for systems returned to service

Industrial facilities evolve over decades. Equipment is upgraded, retrofitted, bypassed, and repurposed. Drawings fall out of date. When something fails, the problem rarely matches the documentation.

Finding the fault requires experience, judgment, and physical verification, not just data.

Training, Certification, and Entry Path

Industrial Electricians typically enter through apprenticeships and trade training, not academic pipelines.

Common pathways include:

- Electrical apprenticeships (often 4 years)
- Union or employer-sponsored training programs
- Transition from maintenance, instrumentation, or military electrical roles

Requirements often include:

- State or provincial electrical licensure
- Safety and lockout/tagout certification

- Ongoing continuing education

Four-year college degrees are not required. Advancement depends on skill breadth, troubleshooting ability, and safety record.

Compensation and Stability

Industrial Electricians earn strong incomes with excellent long-term demand.

- Typical pay range: $70,000–$115,000+ annually
- Higher pay in energy, manufacturing, and hazardous environments
- Overtime common during outages and shutdowns

Skills transferable across industries and regions

Modern industry cannot function without reliable electrical expertise.

Who This Career Is For

This profession is well suited to individuals who:

- Think logically and systematically
- Are comfortable working under pressure
- Take safety seriously without becoming rigid
- Enjoy diagnosing complex problems
- Prefer tangible responsibility over abstraction

It attracts people trusted to restore systems others cannot safely touch.

The Bigger Picture

Industrial Electricians operate at the intersection of power and control. They keep automation honest, machines obedient, and facilities safe.

In discussions about smart factories and autonomous systems, this profession reinforces a core truth running throughout this book:

Someone must understand the system well enough to override it.

Why Industrial Systems Resist Automation

Industrial systems are where plans confront reality. Factories, plants, pipelines, and heavy machinery do not operate in ideal conditions. They run under heat, pressure, vibration, corrosion, contamination, and constant mechanical stress. Components wear unevenly. Materials behave unpredictably. Failures cascade. When something goes wrong, there is no pause button—only diagnosis and intervention.

The professions in this section exist at that boundary.

Heavy equipment field technicians repair machines where they fail, not where it is convenient. Instrumentation technicians ensure that sensors reflect reality rather than fiction. Pipeline operators manage systems where mistakes can be explosive or irreversible. Millwrights align machines to tolerances that software can model but not enforce. Boiler operators control stored energy that tolerates no abstraction. Industrial electricians restore power and control to systems that cannot simply be restarted without consequence.

These roles are not threatened by automation. They enable it.

Modern industry is already heavily automated. The more automated it becomes, the more catastrophic small errors can be. Sensors drift. Control loops misbehave. Interlocks trip. Software responds exactly as programmed—even when the inputs are wrong. At that point, human judgment becomes the last line of defense.

Artificial intelligence can optimize processes and predict failures. It can recommend actions and surface patterns invisible to humans. What it cannot do is take responsibility when those recommendations collide with physical reality. It cannot feel vibration, smell overheating insulation, hear cavitation, or recognize when a machine is about to destroy itself despite "normal" readings.

Industrial systems are also shaped by history. Equipment is layered over decades of upgrades, workarounds, and undocumented modifications. No model fully captures this accumulated complexity. When something behaves unexpectedly, experienced humans interpret the gap between theory and reality.

These professions also reveal a deeper truth about work in an automated age: risk concentrates, it does not disappear. As systems become more efficient, fewer people are needed to operate them—but those people carry far more responsibility. Failure is no longer localized. It propagates.

That responsibility cannot be delegated to software.

Like healthcare and infrastructure, industrial work remains anchored to certification, licensing, and accountability. Someone must sign off. Someone must stand behind a decision to restart a system, reopen a valve, re-energize a circuit, or bring a machine back online.

These careers do not require elite degrees. They require discipline, skill, and the ability to make correct decisions when conditions are imperfect. They reward competence over credentials and experience over abstraction.

As artificial intelligence advances, the most secure work will not be the most digital. It will be the work closest to force, pressure, motion, and failure—where the cost of being wrong is too high to automate away.

Industrial systems resist automation not because technology has failed, but because reality refuses to be simulated completely.

And someone must be trusted to step in when it breaks.

Chapter 5

Environment, Safety, and Regulation: Where Risk Is Managed, Not Eliminated

Modern society does not eliminate risk. It decides where to place it.

Every industrial process, infrastructure system, and economic activity produces byproducts—pollution, hazards, failure modes, and unintended consequences. The professions in this section exist to manage those consequences before they become disasters. They do not create growth. They prevent collapse.

Environmental protection, safety enforcement, and regulatory oversight are often misunderstood as bureaucratic or adversarial. In reality, they are stabilizing forces. They operate where incentives fail, where shortcuts tempt, and where the cost of error is delayed but devastating.

These professions work in the uncomfortable space between what is profitable and what is permissible.

Automation plays a role here, but it does not resolve the central problem. Sensors can detect leaks. Models can estimate exposure. Software can flag violations. What they cannot do is interpret intent, assess real-world conditions, or decide when a rule must be enforced despite pressure to ignore it.

Risk is contextual. Regulations are situational. Enforcement requires judgment.

Environmental systems are especially resistant to abstraction. Ecosystems respond slowly, nonlinearly, and often irreversibly. A miscalculation may not show consequences for years—until remediation is no longer possible. When damage occurs, the question is not which algorithm failed, but who allowed it.

Safety and regulatory roles are also anchored in authority and accountability. Inspectors, compliance officers, and environmental technicians are empowered not because they optimize systems, but because they can stop them. They carry the legal and ethical mandate to say no—to shut down operations, issue citations, halt projects, or demand corrective action.

That authority cannot be automated away.

Like the professions in earlier sections, these roles rarely require elite degrees. They require certification, field knowledge, regulatory fluency, and the willingness to enforce standards under pressure. They reward independence, integrity, and consistency more than speed or innovation.

As artificial intelligence accelerates production and decision-making, the importance of those who slow systems down increases. Someone must ensure that efficiency does not outrun responsibility, and that progress does not externalize its costs onto communities, workers, or the environment.

The chapters that follow examine careers that exist not to build or operate systems—but to contain their risks. They are often invisible, sometimes unpopular, and absolutely necessary.

Because when no one is watching the consequences, someone must be watching the work.

Profile 27

Environmental, Health, and Safety (EHS) Technician

What The Profession Does.

Environmental, Health, and Safety (EHS) Technicians help organizations identify, control, and reduce risks to workers, the public, and the environment. They work in manufacturing plants, construction sites, laboratories, warehouses, energy facilities, and public-sector operations.

Their responsibilities include conducting safety inspections, monitoring environmental conditions, tracking chemical usage, investigating incidents and near-misses, enforcing safety procedures, maintaining regulatory documentation, and training workers on hazard awareness and compliance.

EHS Technicians operate where operations, regulation, and human behavior collide. Their job is not to optimize production—but to prevent injury, illness, contamination, and catastrophe.

Why This Career Survives AI

EHS work is judgment-heavy, adversarial, and accountability-driven—a poor fit for full automation.

AI can assist with data collection, reporting, and trend analysis, but it cannot:

- Perform nuanced, on-site hazard assessments

- Interpret regulatory intent in real-world situations
- Confront unsafe behavior or halt dangerous work
- Balance compliance requirements against operational realities
- Assume legal responsibility for safety decisions

Safety failures rarely occur because data was unavailable. They occur because warnings were ignored, shortcuts were taken, or risks were misjudged. Preventing those outcomes requires human presence, authority, and credibility.

When an incident occurs, investigators do not ask what the software recommended. They ask who allowed the condition to exist.

Training, Certification, and Entry Path

EHS Technician roles are among the most accessible in the safety and regulatory field.

Common entry requirements include:

- High school diploma or GED
- On-the-job training or certificate programs
- OSHA safety training (e.g., OSHA 10/30)

Optional but valuable credentials include:

- CHST (Construction Health and Safety Technician)
- ASP (Associate Safety Professional)
- Environmental compliance or hazardous materials certificates

Four-year degrees are often preferred but not universally required, especially for technician-level roles. Advancement is based on certification, field experience, and regulatory knowledge.

Compensation and Stability

EHS Technicians earn stable incomes with strong long-term demand.

- Typical pay range: $55,000–$85,000+ annually
- Higher pay in energy, construction, and manufacturing
- Daytime schedules common

Demand driven by regulation, insurance, and liability
Regulatory requirements do not disappear during downturns.

Who This Career Is For

This profession is well suited to individuals who:

- Are observant and detail-oriented
- Comfortable enforcing rules and standards
- Can communicate clearly under pressure
- Value prevention over reaction
- Are willing to be unpopular when necessary

It suits people who understand that stopping work

can be the most important work.

The Bigger Picture

EHS Technicians are not obstacles to progress—they are safeguards against its excesses. They ensure that productivity does not outrun responsibility, and that human and environmental costs are not quietly externalized.

In discussions about automation and efficiency, this profession highlights a final, unavoidable truth:

Risk management requires human authority.

Profile 28

Hazardous Materials (HazMat) Technician

What The Profession Does.

Hazardous Materials (HazMat) Technicians respond to incidents involving chemical, biological, radiological, and other dangerous substances that pose risks to people, property, and the environment. They work for fire departments, industrial facilities, environmental response firms, transportation agencies, and government organizations.

Their responsibilities include identifying hazardous substances, assessing exposure risks, containing spills or releases, performing decontamination, monitoring air and surface contamination, and coordinating with emergency responders and regulatory authorities. In industrial settings, they also conduct preventive inspections, maintain response plans, and train personnel in hazardous materials handling.

When something goes wrong with dangerous materials, HazMat Technicians are called because delay makes everything worse.

Why This Career Survives AI

HazMat response exists where uncertainty, danger, and irreversible harm converge.

AI can assist with modeling dispersion, identifying substances, and providing reference data, but it cannot:

- Safely enter contaminated environments
- Perform physical containment and cleanup
- Make judgment calls with incomplete or conflicting information
- Adapt response tactics to rapidly changing conditions
- Accept responsibility for responder and public safety

Hazardous materials incidents rarely unfold according to plan. Labels are missing. Sensors lag. Weather shifts. Secondary reactions occur. Technicians must continuously reassess risk and adjust response strategies in real time.

When lives and ecosystems are at stake, human judgment remains non-negotiable.

Training, Certification, and Entry Path

HazMat Technicians follow structured, certification-based pathways.

Common requirements include:

- High school diploma or GED
- OSHA Hazardous Waste Operations and Emergency Response (HAZWOPER) training
- Employer-sponsored or agency-based HazMat training

Advanced roles may require:

- Fire service HazMat Technician certification
- Specialized chemical, radiological, or industrial

credentials
- Ongoing refresher and recertification training

Four-year degrees are often optional. Advancement depends on certification level, experience, and demonstrated performance under pressure.

Compensation and Stability

HazMat Technicians earn solid incomes with strong long-term demand.

- Typical pay range: $55,000–$90,000+ annually
- Higher pay for emergency response, travel, or specialized materials
- Overtime common during incidents

Demand driven by regulation, transportation, and industrial activity
Hazardous materials do not disappear with automation.

Who This Career Is For

This profession is well suited to individuals who:

- Remain calm in dangerous situations
- Follow procedures precisely while adapting to reality
- Are comfortable wearing protective equipment for long periods

- Value teamwork and disciplined response
- Accept responsibility for high-risk decisions

It attracts people trusted to act when others must retreat.

The Bigger Picture

HazMat Technicians operate at the boundary between control and chaos. Their work prevents accidents from becoming disasters and limits damage when prevention fails.

In conversations about smart systems and automated risk management, this profession delivers a stark reminder:

Some dangers must be faced directly—and by humans.

Profile 29

Environmental Compliance Inspector

What The Profession Does.

Environmental Compliance Inspectors ensure that businesses, municipalities, and industrial facilities follow environmental laws and regulations designed to protect air, water, soil, and public health. They work for government agencies, regulatory bodies, and authorized third-party organizations.

Their duties include conducting site inspections, reviewing permits and records, collecting samples, investigating complaints, documenting violations, and requiring corrective action. Inspectors assess whether operations comply with environmental standards related to emissions, discharges, waste handling, and hazardous materials management.

Their authority exists not to optimize operations—but to draw enforceable boundaries.

Why This Career Survives AI

Environmental compliance work is contextual, adversarial, and legally consequential.

AI can assist with monitoring data and flagging anomalies, but it cannot:

- Conduct comprehensive on-site inspections

- Interpret regulatory intent in complex or ambiguous situations
- Evaluate credibility and cooperation during inspections
- Decide when enforcement action is warranted
- Assume legal responsibility for findings and citations

Environmental violations often occur in gray areas—through neglect, misunderstanding, or deliberate risk-taking. Determining intent, severity, and corrective requirements requires human judgment and authority.

When enforcement decisions are challenged, inspectors—not algorithms—must defend them.

Training, Certification, and Entry Path

Environmental Compliance Inspectors typically enter through experience-based and certification pathways.

Common requirements include:

- High school diploma or GED
- On-the-job training within regulatory agencies
- Technical or environmental compliance training

Many inspectors have backgrounds in:

- Environmental science or technology
- Industrial operations or safety
- Regulatory or enforcement roles

Certifications may be required or preferred

depending on jurisdiction.

Four-year degrees are often helpful but not universally required, especially at technician or inspector levels.

Compensation and Stability

Environmental Compliance Inspectors earn stable, reliable incomes with strong job security.

- Typical pay range: $60,000–$95,000+ annually
- Government positions often include strong benefits
- Daytime schedules common

Demand driven by regulation and public accountability

Environmental law does not suspend itself.

Who This Career Is For

This profession is well suited to individuals who:

- Are observant and methodical
- Comfortable enforcing unpopular rules
- Can communicate clearly and document precisely
- Value public service and integrity
- Prefer authority grounded in law rather than hierarchy

It attracts people willing to say no—and mean it.

The Bigger Picture

Environmental Compliance Inspectors operate at the intersection of economic activity and public consequence. Their work determines whether environmental costs remain contained—or are shifted onto communities and future generations.

In debates about automated monitoring and smart regulation, this profession underscores a fundamental truth:

Rules only matter when someone enforces them.

Profile 30

Industrial Hygiene Technician

What The Profession Does.

Industrial Hygiene Technicians measure, evaluate, and help control workplace exposures that can cause long-term illness or injury. They monitor chemical vapors, dusts, fumes, noise, radiation, heat, and biological agents in industrial, construction, laboratory, and energy environments.

Their work includes air and surface sampling, noise and vibration monitoring, exposure assessments, equipment calibration, and documentation of results for regulatory compliance and risk mitigation. They support industrial hygienists, safety professionals, and regulatory agencies by translating invisible hazards into actionable data.

This is preventive work by design. When it is done well, nothing dramatic happens—years later.

Why This Career Survives AI

Industrial hygiene exists in the space between measurement and interpretation.

AI can assist with data analysis and modeling, but it cannot:

- Perform reliable field sampling under real-world conditions

- Judge whether sampling locations and durations are representative
- Account for human behavior, work practices, and shortcuts
- Interpret exposure results in context
- Decide when risk warrants intervention despite incomplete data

Exposure is not static. It changes with workflow, weather, maintenance quality, and human behavior. Determining whether a hazard is theoretical, acceptable, or dangerous requires human judgment in the field.

Chronic harm does not announce itself. Someone must be trained to look for it.

Training, Certification, and Entry Path

Industrial Hygiene Technician roles are typically certificate- and experience-based.

Common pathways include:

- Technical or vocational programs in industrial hygiene or environmental health
- On-the-job training within safety or compliance teams
- Backgrounds in manufacturing, labs, construction, or environmental work

Relevant credentials may include:

- OSHA training
- Sampling and monitoring certifications
- Progression toward CIH (Certified Industrial

Hygienist) for those who advance

Four-year degrees are often helpful but not required at the technician level. Advancement is based on accuracy, consistency, and regulatory fluency.

Compensation and Stability

Industrial Hygiene Technicians earn stable incomes with long-term demand.

- Typical pay range: $55,000–$85,000+ annually
- Higher pay in energy, manufacturing, and hazardous environments
- Predictable schedules common

Demand driven by regulation, liability, and occupational health awareness

Delayed harm is still harm—and it is regulated accordingly.

Who This Career Is For

This profession is well suited to individuals who:

- Are detail-oriented and methodical
- Comfortable working with data and physical environments
- Prefer prevention over emergency response
- Can communicate risk clearly and credibly
- Value long-term impact over immediate recognition

It attracts people who understand that what you cannot see can still hurt you.

The Bigger Picture

Industrial Hygiene Technicians protect workers from the quiet dangers of modern industry—the exposures that do not cause headlines, but shorten lives. Their work makes productivity compatible with health rather than opposed to it.

In discussions about smart sensors and automated monitoring, this profession reinforces a subtle truth:

Measuring risk is not the same as managing it.

Profile 31

Fire Inspector

What The Profession Does.

Fire Inspectors examine buildings, facilities, and public spaces to ensure compliance with fire codes and life-safety regulations. They work for municipal fire departments, state agencies, insurance authorities, and private inspection organizations.

Their responsibilities include inspecting fire alarms and suppression systems, evaluating means of egress, verifying occupancy limits, reviewing building modifications, investigating fire causes, and issuing citations or stop-use orders when conditions present unacceptable risk.

Fire Inspectors do not respond to emergencies—they work to prevent them. Their authority exists so that fires never reach the point where response is required.

Why This Career Survives AI

Fire inspection is judgment-based, physical, and legally enforceable.

AI can assist with documentation, code references, and scheduling, but it cannot:

- Conduct comprehensive on-site inspections
- Evaluate real-world building use versus permitted use
- Interpret code intent when conditions fall into gray areas
- Confront property owners and require corrective action
- Assume legal responsibility for safety determinations

Fire codes are complex because fire behavior is complex. Inspectors must assess how people actually move through spaces, how materials are stored, and how systems are maintained—not how plans describe them.

When inspectors sign off on a building, they are placing human judgment behind public safety.

Training, Certification, and Entry Path

Fire Inspectors typically enter through certification-driven pathways.

Common routes include:

- Fire service experience
- Construction, electrical, or safety backgrounds
- On-the-job training with fire prevention bureaus

Certifications often include:

- State or municipal fire inspector credentials
- ICC Fire Inspector certification
- NFPA code training

Four-year degrees are often optional. Advancement depends on certification level, experience, and regulatory credibility.

Compensation and Stability

Fire Inspectors earn stable incomes with strong public-sector security.

- Typical pay range: $60,000–$95,000+ annually
- Government benefits common
- Predictable schedules

Demand driven by building density and code enforcement
Fire prevention does not scale down as cities grow.

Who This Career Is For

This profession is well suited to individuals who:

- Are comfortable exercising authority
- Can communicate clearly and firmly
- Understand building systems and human behavior
- Value prevention over reaction
- Accept responsibility for unpopular decisions

It suits people who understand that stopping unsafe use can save lives.

The Bigger Picture

Fire Inspectors operate at a crucial threshold: the point where risk becomes unacceptable. Their work prevents tragedies that only become visible when inspection fails.

In discussions about smart buildings and automated safety systems, this profession reinforces a final truth for Part IV:

Life-safety still requires a human willing to enforce limits.

Why Safety and Regulation Resist Automation

Safety and regulation exist because incentives fail. Left to efficiency alone, systems drift toward risk. Shortcuts accumulate. Margins thin. Hazards are tolerated until something breaks—or someone is harmed. The professions in this section exist to interrupt that drift, to enforce limits where economic pressure encourages overreach.

Environmental, health, and safety work is not about prediction. It is about intervention.

EHS Technicians identify hazards before they cause harm. Industrial hygiene technicians measure exposures that do not announce themselves until years later. Hazardous materials technicians respond when prevention fails and containment becomes urgent. Environmental compliance inspectors enforce boundaries after voluntary compliance has run its course. Fire inspectors ensure that life-safety systems are ready for the moment no one wants to imagine.

These roles operate where uncertainty is high and tolerance for error is low.

Artificial intelligence can monitor, model, and analyze. It can estimate risk and flag anomalies. What it cannot do is confront unsafe behavior, interpret intent, or exercise authority in contested spaces. It cannot decide when a violation is serious enough to stop work, issue a citation, evacuate a building, or escalate enforcement despite resistance.

Risk management is not a technical problem alone. It is a human one.

Environmental and safety failures rarely occur because no one had data. They occur because warnings were ignored, tradeoffs were misjudged, or responsibility was diluted. These professions exist to concentrate responsibility—to make sure someone is empowered, identifiable, and accountable.

Regulation also exposes a misconception about automation: that more monitoring leads to less oversight. In practice, increased data often demands more judgment. Sensors report numbers, not meaning. Compliance requires interpretation. Enforcement requires authority. When consequences arrive years later or miles away, someone must still answer for the decision to allow risk in the first place.

Like the professions in earlier sections, these roles do not require elite credentials. They require training, certification, regulatory fluency, and the willingness to act under pressure. They reward integrity over speed and judgment over optimization.

As artificial intelligence accelerates production, extraction, and decision-making, the importance of those who slow systems down increases. Someone must ensure that progress does not externalize its costs—onto workers, communities, or the environment.

Safety and regulation resist automation not because technology is insufficient, but because accountability cannot be delegated.

When harm occurs, society does not ask what the model predicted. It asks who allowed the risk to exist.

And someone must be willing to answer.

Chapter 6

Logistics, Movement, and System Controls: Where Flow Is Everything

Modern life depends less on what is produced than on what continues to move.

Food, fuel, medicine, raw materials, data, and people must arrive where they are needed—on time, in the correct condition, and in the correct sequence. When movement stalls, shortages appear immediately. When coordination fails, abundance becomes useless.

The professions in this section operate inside that reality. They manage the flow of goods, energy, vehicles, and information across tightly coupled systems where delay, misrouting, or miscommunication can cascade into systemic failure. Their work is not glamorous. It is synchronizing.

Logistics is often described as a software problem. In practice, it is a physical control problem. Vehicles break down. Weather intervenes. Infrastructure degrades. Humans behave unpredictably. Automated systems optimize for normal conditions; experienced operators manage the exceptions.

These careers sit at the intersection of planning and execution. They translate schedules into movement, manifests into action, and control signals into real-world behavior. When systems drift out of alignment, they intervene—not by rewriting code, but by rerouting, rescheduling, isolating, or shutting down components to prevent wider disruption.

Artificial intelligence plays a growing role in forecasting, routing, and optimization. But logistics systems are only as resilient as their human overseers. When models conflict, data lags, or conditions change faster than software can adapt, human judgment restores coherence.

Like the professions in earlier sections, these roles are anchored in accountability. Someone must decide which shipment moves first during a shortage, which train waits on a siding, which aircraft remains grounded, or which system is throttled to protect downstream operations. These decisions carry economic, safety, and sometimes life-and-death consequences.

Many of these careers do not require four-year degrees. They require situational awareness, procedural discipline, and the ability to think several steps ahead under pressure. They reward people who can see the system as a whole—and act decisively when it begins to slip.

As automation accelerates, movement does not become simpler. It becomes more fragile. The faster and leaner systems run, the less margin they have for error.

The chapters that follow examine professions that keep modern society in motion. They do not eliminate friction. They manage it.

Because when flow stops, everything else follows.

Profile 32

Railroad Dispatcher

What The Profession Does.

Railroad Dispatchers control the movement of trains across vast rail networks, coordinating freight and passenger traffic to ensure safe, efficient, and timely operations. From centralized control centers, they authorize train movements, assign track usage, manage meet-and-pass decisions, and respond to delays, failures, and emergencies.

Dispatchers monitor train locations, signal systems, track conditions, maintenance windows, and crew availability. They must constantly balance competing priorities: on-time performance, safety, infrastructure limits, and unexpected disruptions. Every decision affects not just one train, but the flow of the entire network.

Trains do not steer themselves. Someone must decide who moves, who waits, and why.

Why This Career Survives AI

Rail dispatching is high-stakes, real-time system coordination under imperfect conditions.

AI can assist with scheduling, optimization, and predictive modeling, but it cannot:

- Resolve conflicting priorities during cascading disruptions

- Adapt plans when infrastructure, crews, or equipment fail unexpectedly
- Exercise conservative judgment when safety margins narrow
- Communicate and coordinate with human crews in evolving situations
- Accept responsibility for collisions, derailments, or near-misses

Rail networks are intentionally constrained. Tracks are shared. Sidings are finite. Delays propagate. When conditions diverge from plan—as they frequently do—dispatchers must improvise within strict safety rules.

Automation proposes. Dispatchers decide.

Training, Certification, and Entry Path

Railroad Dispatchers typically enter through employer-based training programs, not academic pipelines.

Common requirements include:

- High school diploma or GED
- Intensive classroom and simulation training
- Qualification on specific territories and rulesets

Training covers:

- Railroad operating rules
- Signal systems and track layouts
- Emergency procedures
- Communication protocols

Four-year degrees are not required. Dispatchers

advance through territory qualification, experience, and demonstrated judgment under pressure.

Compensation and Stability

Railroad Dispatchers earn strong incomes with exceptional job security.

- Typical pay range: $70,000–$120,000+ annually
- Shift work, nights, and weekends common
- Union representation in many systems

Demand tied to freight movement and passenger rail operations

Railroads cannot outsource or automate away dispatch authority.

Who This Career Is For

This profession is well suited to individuals who:

- Think systemically and several moves ahead
- Remain calm during cascading disruptions
- Communicate clearly and decisively
- Are comfortable with responsibility for large-scale outcomes
- Prefer control rooms to field work

It rewards people trusted to make the least bad decision when no perfect option exists.

The Bigger Picture

Railroad Dispatchers operate the circulatory system of ground transportation. When dispatching works, goods arrive, commuters move, and supply chains remain intact. When it fails, everything downstream suffers.

In conversations about autonomous transport and smart networks, this profession underscores a central truth of Chapter 6: Flow requires judgment.

Profile 33

Air Traffic Controller

What The Profession Does.

Air Traffic Controllers (ATCs) manage the safe and orderly movement of aircraft through controlled airspace and on airport surfaces. Working in control towers, approach facilities, and en route centers, they sequence takeoffs and landings, maintain aircraft separation, issue routing instructions, and respond to weather, mechanical issues, and emergencies in real time.

Controllers monitor multiple aircraft simultaneously, tracking altitude, speed, heading, and intent while coordinating with pilots, adjacent facilities, and ground operations. Every instruction must be precise, timely, and unambiguous. There is no rewind, and no pause.

When air traffic control works, aviation is one of the safest modes of transport ever created. When it fails, consequences are immediate and catastrophic.

Why This Career Survives AI

Air traffic control is real-time, safety-critical decision-making under uncertainty—a domain where automation assists but cannot replace humans.

AI can assist with conflict detection, traffic flow

management, and weather modeling, but it cannot:

- Exercise conservative judgment when multiple risks collide
- Adapt instantly to novel, cascading failures
- Communicate nuance and urgency to human pilots
- Resolve ambiguity when data is incomplete or contradictory
- Accept responsibility for loss of life

Aircraft do not move in isolation. Weather cells shift. Pilots misunderstand instructions. Equipment degrades. Emergencies overlap. When plans unravel, controllers must prioritize, improvise within strict rules, and maintain safety margins that no algorithm can fully guarantee.

Automation proposes options. Controllers decide what is safe.

Training, Certification, and Entry Path

Air Traffic Controllers enter through one of the most rigorous non-degree training pipelines in modern work.

Typical requirements include:

- U.S. citizenship (for FAA roles)
- Passing aptitude, medical, and background screening
- Completion of FAA-approved training or military ATC experience

Training involves:

- Intensive classroom instruction

- High-fidelity simulation
- On-the-job certification at assigned facilities

Four-year degrees are not required. Qualification depends on performance under pressure, not academic pedigree. Not everyone who starts finishes.

Compensation and Stability

Air Traffic Controllers earn high incomes with exceptional job security.

- Typical pay range: $90,000–$180,000+ annually
- Federal benefits and retirement systems
- Mandatory retirement age due to cognitive demands
- Demand tied to air traffic volume and national safety

The system cannot function without certified human controllers.

Who This Career Is For

This profession is well suited to individuals who:

- Process information rapidly and accurately
- Remain calm under intense pressure
- Communicate decisively and clearly
- Accept responsibility for irreversible outcomes
- Prefer mastery and consequence over comfort

It is demanding, unforgiving, and deeply consequential work.

The Bigger Picture

Air Traffic Controllers operate the most unforgiving flow system in modern society: three-dimensional movement at speed, with no physical buffers. Their work demonstrates the outer limit of automation's reach.

In discussions about autonomous aircraft and AI-managed skies, this profession delivers one of the clearest lessons in the book:

When failure means lives lost instantly, humans remain in control.

Profile 34

Port Operations Coordinator

What The Profession Does.

Port Operations Coordinators manage the movement of ships, cargo, equipment, and personnel within seaports and marine terminals. They coordinate vessel arrivals and departures, berth assignments, crane operations, container flows, yard logistics, and intermodal transfers to rail and truck networks.

Working from operations centers and terminal offices, coordinators synchronize shipping schedules, labor availability, equipment status, customs requirements, and weather conditions. They serve as the connective tissue between shipping lines, stevedores, pilots, tug operators, railroads, trucking companies, and port authorities.

Ports do not move quickly—but they move continuously. Coordination failures ripple through global supply chains.

Why This Career Survives AI

Port operations are multi-actor, multi-constraint, and delay-intolerant.

AI can assist with scheduling, forecasting, and optimization, but it cannot:

- Resolve conflicts between competing

stakeholders in real time

- Adapt plans when labor actions, weather, or equipment failures intervene
- Prioritize safety, security, and throughput under pressure
- Coordinate human crews across shifting conditions
- Accept responsibility for congestion, accidents, or missed sailings

Ports are hybrid environments—part industrial site, part transportation hub, part regulatory zone. Conditions change hourly. Equipment breaks. Crews rotate. Ships arrive late. When plans collapse, human coordinators re-establish flow.

Automation suggests efficiency. Coordinators preserve continuity.

Training, Certification, and Entry Path

Port Operations Coordinators typically enter through experience-based pathways, not academic pipelines.

Common backgrounds include:

- Terminal operations or yard supervision
- Maritime, logistics, or transportation roles
- Military logistics or port security experience

Requirements often include:

- On-the-job training in terminal systems and procedures
- Knowledge of maritime safety and security regulations

- Familiarity with intermodal logistics

Four-year degrees are sometimes preferred but not universally required. Advancement depends on situational awareness, communication skill, and operational judgment.

Compensation and Stability

Port Operations Coordinators earn solid incomes with strong long-term demand.

- Typical pay range: $60,000–$100,000+ annually
- Shift work common in busy ports
- Strong employment stability tied to trade volume
- Skills transferable across ports and logistics hubs

Global trade does not digitize away physical ports.

Who This Career Is For

This profession is well suited to individuals who:

- Think in systems rather than tasks
- Can juggle multiple priorities under time pressure
- Communicate clearly across organizations
- Are comfortable making tradeoffs with incomplete information
- Prefer coordination over command

It rewards people who keep complex systems moving without needing to be seen.

The Bigger Picture

Port Operations Coordinators manage one of the most critical choke points in global civilization. Food, energy, medicine, and manufactured goods all pass through spaces where delays compound and mistakes echo worldwide.

In discussions about automated supply chains and frictionless trade, this profession delivers a grounded reminder:

Movement at scale still requires human coordination.

Profile 35

SCADA / Control Room Operator (Supervisory Control and Data Acquisition Operator)

What The Profession Does.

SCADA Operators monitor and control complex, distributed systems from centralized control rooms. These systems include electric grids, water and wastewater networks, pipelines, transit systems, manufacturing processes, and other critical infrastructure.

Using real-time data feeds, alarms, and control interfaces, operators regulate flows, pressures, voltages, temperatures, and system states across wide geographic areas. They start and stop equipment, isolate faults, coordinate field crews, and respond to abnormal conditions that could escalate into outages, environmental damage, or safety incidents.

SCADA Operators do not merely watch screens. They intervene, often under time pressure, when automated systems encounter conditions they were not designed to handle.

Why This Career Survives AI

SCADA systems are already highly automated.

That is precisely why human operators remain essential.

AI can assist with optimization, forecasting, and anomaly detection, but it cannot:

- Decide which alarms matter during cascading failures
- Balance competing priorities across interconnected systems
- Adapt safely when sensors fail or data conflicts
- Coordinate human field crews during emergencies
- Accept responsibility for system-wide consequences

Automated control works well under normal conditions. Real crises are not normal. Alarms cascade. Data lags. Models disagree. When systems begin to drift toward failure, operators restore coherence by applying judgment, experience, and restraint.

Automation executes. Humans decide when to override it.

Training, Certification, and Entry Path

SCADA Operators typically enter through technical and operational pathways, not academic ones.

Common entry routes include:

- On-the-job training within utilities or industrial facilities
- Backgrounds in operations, instrumentation, electrical, or process control
- Military or industrial control experience

Training focuses on:

- System behavior and failure modes
- Control logic and safety interlocks
- Emergency response procedures
- Communication and escalation protocols

Four-year degrees are often optional. Qualification depends on demonstrated competence under supervision, not credentials.

Compensation and Stability

SCADA Operators earn strong incomes with exceptional job stability.

- Typical pay range: $65,000–$110,000+ annually
- Shift work common, including nights and weekends
- High demand across utilities, energy, water, and transportation.
- Skills transferable across sectors

Critical systems cannot be left unattended.

Who This Career Is For

This profession is well suited to individuals who:

- Think calmly during complex failures
- Can prioritize under information overload
- Trust procedures without becoming rigid
- Communicate clearly during emergencies
- Accept responsibility for large, invisible systems

It rewards people who understand that doing nothing at the wrong moment can be as dangerous as doing the wrong thing.

The Bigger Picture

SCADA Operators sit at the nerve centers of modern civilization. Power, water, fuel, transportation, and production all pass through systems they oversee. When everything works, no one notices. When it doesn't, their decisions determine whether disruption is contained—or spreads.

In conversations about autonomous systems and smart infrastructure, this profession delivers one of the book's clearest conclusions:

Automation still requires someone to be in charge.

Profile 36

Transportation Operations Coordinator

What The Profession Does.

Transportation Operations Coordinators oversee the real-time movement of vehicles, crews, and cargo across transportation networks. They work in trucking companies, transit agencies, logistics firms, distribution centers, and public transportation systems.

Their responsibilities include dispatching vehicles, adjusting routes, managing schedules, responding to breakdowns or delays, coordinating with drivers and maintenance teams, and communicating with customers, terminals, and regulators. When conditions change—weather, traffic, equipment failure, labor shortages—coordinators adapt plans to keep systems moving.

They do not design networks. They keep them functioning.

Why This Career Survives AI

Transportation coordination is exception-driven work.

AI can optimize routes and schedules under normal conditions, but it cannot:

- Resolve cascading disruptions across multiple carriers or modes

- Balance service commitments against safety and regulatory constraints
- Communicate effectively with drivers, crews, and field supervisors
- Make judgment calls when data is late, wrong, or incomplete
- Accept responsibility for delays, accidents, or service failures

Transportation systems fail in human ways: missed handoffs, unclear instructions, weather surprises, mechanical issues, and behavioral variability. When optimization breaks down, human coordinators restore order.

Software plans. Coordinators adapt.

Training, Certification, and Entry Path

Transportation Operations Coordinators typically enter through experience-based pathways.

Common backgrounds include:

- Dispatch or fleet operations
- Warehousing or distribution roles
- Transit or logistics support positions
- Military transportation or logistics experience

Requirements often include:

- On-the-job training in dispatch and tracking systems
- Familiarity with transportation regulations and safety rules
- Strong communication and organizational skills

Four-year degrees are sometimes preferred but rarely required. Advancement depends on situational awareness, reliability, and decision-making under pressure.

Compensation and Stability

Transportation Operations Coordinators earn steady incomes with persistent demand.

- Typical pay range: $55,000–$90,000+ annually
- Shift work common in 24/7 operations
- Demand tied to freight movement, transit systems, and supply chains

Skills transferable across industries and regions
Goods and people do not move themselves.

Who This Career Is For

This profession is well suited to individuals who:

- Think quickly and pragmatically
- Can manage competing priorities without panic
- Communicate clearly and calmly
- Prefer coordination over direct authority
- Take responsibility for keeping things moving

It rewards people who excel at damage control and recovery, not perfection.

The Bigger Picture

Transportation Operations Coordinators keep modern life synchronized. They absorb disruption so that the rest of society experiences continuity. When systems are stressed, they decide what moves first, what waits, and what must be rerouted.

In conversations about autonomous vehicles and algorithmic logistics, this profession reinforces a central lesson of Chapter 6: Movement depends on human judgment when plans fail.

Why Flow and Control Resist Automation

Modern society is not held together by production alone, but by coordination.

Goods must arrive before they are needed. Vehicles must not collide. Systems must remain synchronized across distance, time, and uncertainty. When flow breaks, scarcity appears immediately—even in a world of abundance. The professions in this section exist to prevent that break.

Railroad dispatchers, air traffic controllers, port operations coordinators, SCADA operators, and transportation operations coordinators all work in environments where plans rarely survive contact with reality. Weather intervenes. Equipment fails. Crews arrive late. Data lags or conflicts. Under these conditions, efficiency matters less than coherence.

Automation already plays a major role in logistics and control. Schedules are optimized. Routes are calculated. Conflicts are flagged. But automated systems assume normal conditions. Real systems spend much of their time outside that envelope.

When disruption cascades, someone must decide what moves first, what waits, what reroutes, and what stops entirely. These are not technical decisions alone. They are judgments that balance safety, fairness, downstream impact, and irreversibility.

Artificial intelligence can propose solutions. It cannot own consequences.

Flow systems are also unforgiving of delay. In healthcare, seconds matter. In infrastructure, hours matter. In logistics, timing is everything. A missed slot, a delayed handoff, or a misprioritized movement can ripple through entire regions or industries. Recovering from disruption requires anticipation, communication, and authority—qualities that remain human.

These professions expose a subtle truth about automation: the faster and leaner systems become, the less margin they have for error. Optimization reduces slack. Slack absorbs failure. When slack disappears, judgment becomes critical.

Like the roles in earlier sections, these careers do not rely on elite credentials. They rely on trust, training, and the demonstrated ability to think several steps ahead under pressure. They reward people who can remain calm while managing complexity—and who accept responsibility for outcomes they cannot fully control.

As artificial intelligence accelerates movement and coordination, the most secure work will not be at the edges of systems, but at their control points. Someone must be empowered to intervene when automated logic collides with physical reality.

Flow resists automation not because technology is inadequate, but because systems fail in ways that cannot be precomputed.

When everything is moving, no one notices. When movement falters, everything else follows.

And someone must decide how to restore it.

Chapter 7

Second Acts and Sustainable Careers Who Are These Professions For?

The professions in this book are not for everyone—and that is precisely why they endure.

They do not promise prestige, rapid wealth, or public recognition. They do not reward constant self-promotion. They do not scale easily or lend themselves to personal branding. What they offer instead is something rarer: usefulness that persists.

These careers are well suited to people at inflection points—those reassessing not just how they work, but why.

Many readers arrive here after a first act that did not unfold as planned. Some have been displaced by automation, consolidation, or outsourcing. Others are simply tired of work that feels abstract, fragile, or detached from real consequence. Some have degrees they no longer use. Others avoided debt and now seek stability without stagnation.

This section is for them.

These professions tend to attract people who value responsibility over recognition. People who prefer being trusted to being visible. People who are comfortable knowing that their best days end with nothing dramatic happening—because that means the system held.

They also suit those who want boundaries. Unlike many modern careers, these roles have clear definitions of success: the patient stabilizes, the power stays on, the system remains within limits, the shipment arrives safely. Work ends when the shift ends. Responsibility is real—but it is not endless.

Importantly, these careers do not require starting over intellectually. They reward maturity. Judgment improves with age. Calm under pressure matters more than speed. Many of these roles are filled by second-career workers, veterans, tradespeople transitioning into oversight roles, and professionals leaving purely cognitive work for something grounded.

They are also well suited to people who are not anti-technology, but realistic about it. The individuals in these roles work with advanced systems every day. They understand automation deeply—often better than its advocates—because they are the ones who intervene when it fails.

What unites these professions is not skillset, sector, or temperament. It is a shared relationship to consequence. Errors matter. Success is quiet. Accountability is unavoidable.

For readers seeking reinvention without reinvention theater—for work that does not require constant reinvention of the self—these careers offer a different promise: a second act built on reliability rather than reinvention.

They are not immune to change. But they are anchored to realities that change slowly: human bodies, physical systems, risk, movement, and responsibility.

In a world that increasingly rewards novelty, these professions reward continuity.

And for many people, especially in a second act, that is not a compromise. It is the point.

Why These Careers Hold Up Over Time

Most careers are designed around growth. These careers are designed around continuity.

The difference matters. Growth assumes expansion, acceleration, and novelty. Continuity assumes maintenance, judgment, and endurance. The professions in this book belong to the second category—and that is why they age well.

They persist because the problems they address do not go away. People continue to get sick. Infrastructure continues to degrade. Machines continue to fail. Risk continues to accumulate. Goods must continue to move. None of these realities depend on market trends or consumer preference. They are structural features of modern life.

This gives these careers a form of durability that is increasingly rarc.

Unlike roles built around platforms, branding, or proprietary tools, these professions are portable. Licenses, certifications, and experience can travel. A water operator, dispatcher, safety technician, or control room operator can relocate without abandoning their profession. Skills are transferable because the underlying systems—water, power, transport, regulation—are universal.

They also resist skill obsolescence. While tools evolve, the core competencies remain stable: situational awareness, procedural discipline, risk assessment, and judgment under pressure. A veteran operator is often more valuable than a newly trained one precisely because experience compounds rather than expires.

These careers are also bounded. There is an upper limit to responsibility, and a clear understanding of when work ends. Unlike many knowledge-economy roles, they do not demand constant availability, personal brand maintenance, or identity fusion with work. This makes them sustainable not just economically, but psychologically.

Importantly, they offer predictable progression rather than explosive upside. Pay increases come from certification levels, seniority, and responsibility—not from outperforming peers or capturing attention. For second-act workers, this predictability is a feature, not a flaw.

They are also resilient to economic cycles. Societies may delay projects, reduce hours, or slow hiring—but they cannot suspend water treatment, emergency response, system control, or safety enforcement. These functions are among the last to be eliminated and the first to be restored.

Finally, these careers align well with aging. They reward calm over speed, accuracy over volume, and judgment over novelty. Many allow workers to transition from physical to supervisory or control roles over time, extending employability without forcing reinvention.

In an economy increasingly optimized for youth, flexibility, and constant adaptation, these professions offer something different: careers that improve with experience.

For those thinking in decades rather than quarters, that may be the most sustainable feature of all.

What These Careers Demand—and What They Don't

The professions in this book make real demands. They are not passive roles, and they are not easy work disguised as stability. What distinguishes them is not a lack of difficulty, but the kind of difficulty they require.

They demand attention. Many of these roles involve long periods where nothing appears to be happening—followed by moments when everything matters at once. The ability to remain alert, patient, and disciplined when systems are stable is as important as decisive action when they are not.

They demand responsibility. In these careers, there is often a named individual on shift, on duty, or on call. Decisions are traceable. Outcomes are owned. This can be stressful—but it is also clarifying. Work has edges. Accountability is explicit.

They demand respect for procedure without blindness to reality. Rules exist because failure has consequences, but rigid adherence without judgment can be as dangerous as improvisation without discipline. These roles require people who know when to follow the book and when to recognize that the book cannot cover everything.

They demand comfort with invisibility. Success is quiet. When things go right, no one notices. When they go wrong, attention is immediate and often unforgiving. There is little public credit for prevention.

They demand ethical steadiness. Many of these professionals operate under pressure to hurry, overlook, or defer enforcement. Doing the right thing may mean stopping work, delaying schedules, or creating friction. Integrity is not optional.

Just as important is what these careers do not demand.

They do not require constant reinvention. Mastery is cumulative. Skills deepen rather than expire. You are not expected to rebrand yourself every few years.

They do not demand ideological alignment or cultural performance. Competence matters more than opinion. Results matter more than rhetoric.

They do not require prestige credentials. While training, certification, and licensing are real, they are targeted. What counts is whether you can be trusted to do the work when it matters.

They do not require your identity. You are not expected to love the job, evangelize it, or turn it into a lifestyle. You are expected to perform it well, hand off responsibly, and go home.

For many people in a second act, these tradeoffs are not limitations. They are relief.

These careers exchange excitement for endurance, recognition for trust, and novelty for usefulness. They are not for those seeking constant affirmation or unlimited upside.

They are for those who want to know—clearly and honestly—that their work still matters.

Chapter 8

Choosing Work That Endures

The future of work is often described as a race: faster skills, faster tools, faster adaptation. That framing is incomplete.

The professions in this book tell a different story. They reveal an economy that does not run on novelty alone, but on continuity—on people who show up, take responsibility, and keep systems within safe bounds when no one is watching.

These careers endure not because they resist technology, but because they sit where technology meets reality. Bodies still fail. Machines still break. Infrastructure still degrades. Risk still accumulates. Goods still need to move. When automated systems encounter conditions they were not designed to handle, someone must intervene.

That intervention is human.

What connects the hidden professions you've just explored is not sector, status, or education level. It is accountability. In each case, a real person is trusted to make decisions with irreversible consequences. That trust cannot be abstracted away.

This has implications for anyone navigating an uncertain economic landscape.

If your goal is speed, prestige, or speculative upside, these careers may disappoint. They do not promise constant excitement or exponential growth. They do not reward visibility or self-promotion.

If your goal is durability, they offer something better.

They offer work that remains necessary regardless of trends. Work that is bounded rather than endless. Work where experience compounds rather than expires. Work that allows a life outside of constant reinvention.

They are particularly well suited to second acts—not as consolation prizes, but as informed choices. Many people arrive at this stage with sharper judgment, steadier nerves, and clearer values. These professions reward exactly that.

This book does not argue that everyone should pursue these paths. It argues that they deserve to be visible—and taken seriously—at a time when many people are being told, implicitly or explicitly, that their usefulness has an expiration date.

It does not.

Society will always need people who can be trusted with systems that cannot fail quietly.

As artificial intelligence accelerates change, the most resilient work will not be the most abstract. It will be the work anchored to consequence—where mistakes matter, responsibility is explicit, and success looks like continuity rather than disruption.

Choosing such work is not settling.

It is choosing to be necessary.

And in an uncertain future, necessity endures.

Made in United States
Troutdale, OR
11/03/2026

56518900R00126